Public WORKS

six decades of writing and
reading out loud

Bill Mann

Interior Art by Susanne Sherer

Graphic Designs by Artline Graphics, Sedona, Arizona

Covers Collaborated by
Anugito ten Voorde and Susanne Sherer

Copyright © 2017 by Bill Mann

Double Chin Publishing
P.O. Box 20428
Sedona, Arizona 86341
authorbillmann@gmail.com

ISBN-13: 978-1548073145
ISBN-10: 1548073148

All rights reserved. No part of this book may be used or reproduced in any manner whatsoever without written permission, except in the case of brief quotations and appropriate citations for the purpose of critical articles and reviews.

For Susanne Sherer,

mother of all muses,

who united my past,

my present,

and my future.

12.14.17

use imagination!

Susanne Sherer

Acknowledgements

Susanne Sherer, the provocative abstract expressionist artist, married her imagery to the multitude of literary themes included here, under the most challenging circumstances.

Cassandra Nicholson word processed a labyrinth of hand written poems, technically stitching together the entire body of this book.

Anugito ten Voorde of Artline Graphics, has designed all of the author's books, forever displaying limitless perfection and imagination.

"Ahado!" (Limitless)

T A B L E   O F

Introduction	9
Poetic Beginnings	15
(feeling my way through adolescence and youth)	
Towards Life in General	71
For Love and Lovers	119
Dissonance and Discontent	197
Slam Poetry	247
Freestyle/Rapid Fire	253
Song Lyrics	265
Obits	285

CONTENTS

Lucid Dreamer	317
Two American Pastimes	318
The Sounds of Baseball	320
Getting Things Done vs. Who We Are	322
Time Delayed Exposure	325
Here We Go Again	328
Menudo	330
Jeff Bridges	332
The Eric Schmidt Dilemma	333
Long Lost Good Friend Steve Chesney	335
Chesney and Julie	336
No Name, No Place	340
The Ravens, The Real Estate, The Room, The Roof	341
Children's Stories	345
Paula Goes To The Pound	347
Sarah's Voice	354
Saving The World From Boredom	358
The Dog That Rode Horses	360
Tiny Templeton	363
What Does Bear Do In The Woods?	368
Bird. Wind. Tree.	372

Introduction

It is safe to say that no person ever learned to adequately speak a new language without reading certain things out loud. Reading out loud magically transforms the written word. The material begins as something passive, on the order of television. But the moment the reader is called upon to "stand and deliver," the act of reading out loud activates the 'one way' experience into an enlivening event for both the reader and the audience.

This I have been doing, since my first poem to my mother, at the age of five. Encouraged by this, I then ambushed my father and his fellow auto parts workers with a blush-worthy birthday poem. Then it was on to my high school beer-bingeing buddies, and later to the inmates in two different mental institutions.

Multitudes of dogs and cats probably wished they could cover their ears. And when no greater creatures were available, I read out loud to the mirror, and to the fly on the mirror on the wall. Mostly good outcomes (including real social change) came from these spirited outbursts of the items offered here in "Public Works."

A few years ago, I attended the Napa Chapter of the California Writers Association's monthly reading by various authors, followed by questions and critiques.

At about the same time, renowned poet Robert Eastwood and the Danville California Poets Society invited me to recite two of my poems at one of their regular round table readings, occurring at the home of fellow poet Jan Hersh.

This was preceded and followed by creative readings in Canada, Mexico, Portugal and Spain – as well as at several U.S. book festivals. Along the way, I was fortunate to co-own the Old Monterey Book Company, whose rich literary history included hauntings by a previous generation of 'Beat' poets and writers. The store's 24-hour coffee pot and a book-loving cat named 'Hoover' attracted a lively crust of storytellers, including famed photographer Ansel Adams, and Richard Byrd, great-grandson of the legendary South Pole explorer Admiral Richard Evelyn Byrd.

I also enjoyed a reading encounter with Allen Ginsberg during one of his stays in Carmel, California, and spent some inspired evenings at Lawrence Ferlinghetti's City Lights Book Store in North Beach, San Francisco. However, it was the sheer intensity of the Napa/Danville oral events, which firmed my resolution to publish a life's habit of imposing on others through the act of reading out loud. That moment cast the basis for the title, "Public Works."

Some audiences have been tougher on this bard than others. During my early twenties, while working as a psychiatric aid, I was asked by a patient to read out loud whatever I was carrying around with me at the time. In

the visitors lounge, I belted out pithy morsels of
Gurdjieff, Henry Miller, Ayn Rand, Nietzsche, and
Thomas Aquinas. These barely aroused a pulse.

Finally, a pair of limericks managed to save my asylum
act from completely bombing. To the chagrin of hospital
staff, the patient population then took up the limerick
craze in earnest. Years later, I also suffered a rough bunch
of Taiwanese Karaoke Club mad men, who booed me
from finishing my singing of a Stephen Foster lullaby.
("Beel, you terabal.")

Most recently among my flops, an active Arizona
children's library set out to determine if a passionate
reader like myself could hold the attention of a room full
of two-year-olds. Everyone knows the answer to that
one!

These anecdotes are offered as part of my undeterred
belief that "to find your voice you first need to hear your
voice." Hearing your voice may help you to keep it close
at hand, uncovering an even better sense of self.

Standing back from my life out loud as expressed in
these offerings of poetry, prose, dreams, and song lyrics –
I have subjectively discovered the following truths:

> I still love.
> I still lust.
> I still write.
> I am forever a child.
> I am mindful as an adult.

I trust myself.
I am in touch.
I desire to learn.
I know how to recreate.
I am on good terms with nature.

"Public Works" represents the unbreakable binding and all the threads that have kept me sanely and socially connected. Reading out loud has saved me from simply being an observer. I encourage you with all the love and truth inside of me – to please give it a try!

Bill Mann
July 2017

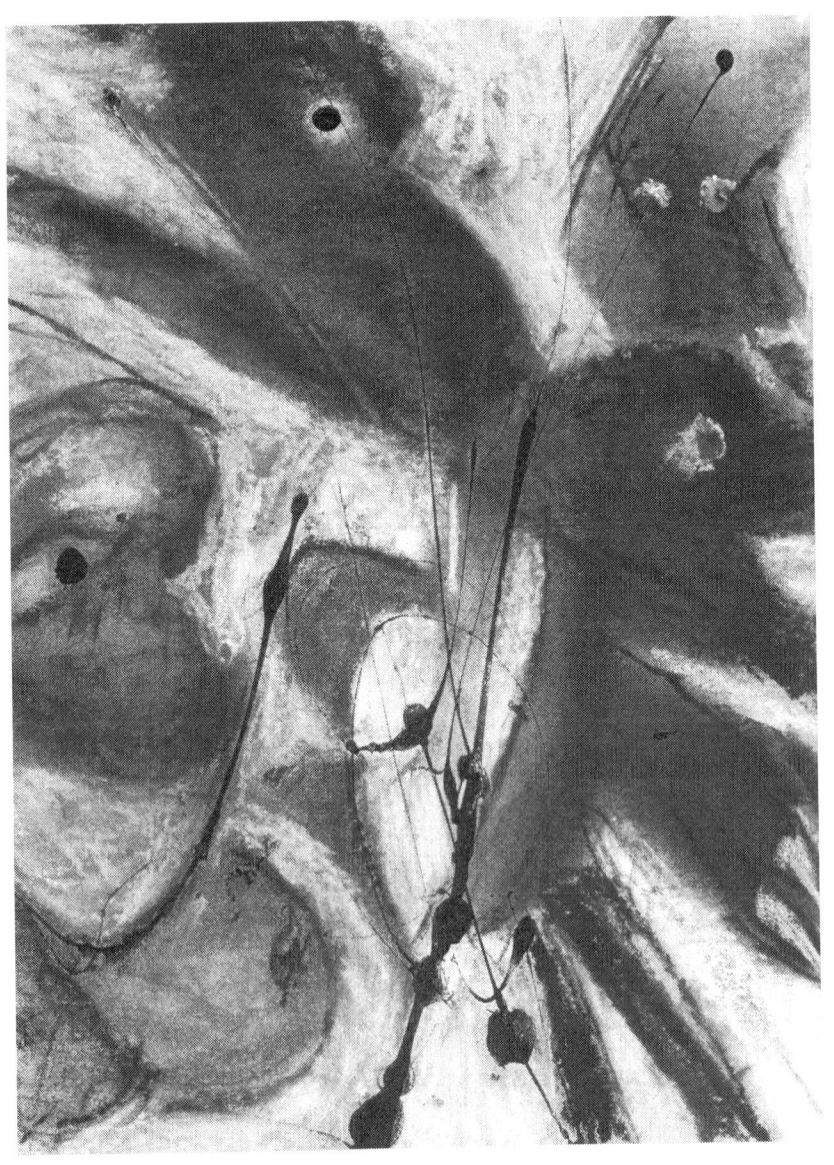

1
Poetic Beginnings

Feeling my way through
adolescence and youth

Age 5 to Age 20

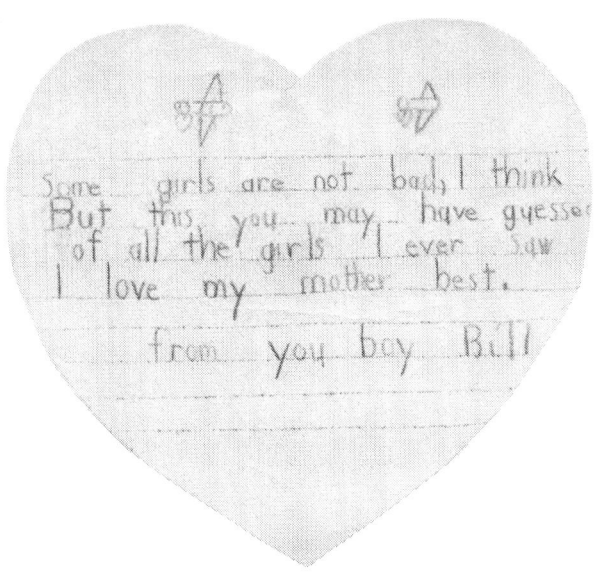

MOST POETS WHOM I have met refer to their embarrassing early poems as "crap." Beneath the shudders of self-loathing regarding their first creations, these same writers seldom trash their starry-eyed drivel. I am no exception.

Many of the following items made their way back to me after living in a Midwestern barn, amongst the spiders and dust mites for more than 30 years. The poems are lanky and raw. I did not have the heart to edit them.

I cling to them like so many meridians to my youth.

The Learning Process

We left the bubble-gum crowd
chewing nonchalantly,
not too concerned
with life's atrocities – not at all.
Curiosity pushed us
to look at harsh realities
through books and beer bottles
and PhD's and letters home;
discussions, entangling
us in all the sound
and fury that 'Shake'
called ignorance,
plus the opposite sex,
who wrote their moral codes
and were frustrated
accordingly.
Guess ol' God or Somebody
put us on this earth
to make decisions
and grow up hoping
that Charlie Chapman
would sweep us up and gone
to walk with him
to NOWHERE!

For S

AS FAR AS he was concerned...
he had a lot.
He had heart and he knew it,
because when SHE RODE WITH HIM
it made him short-winded...
but stronger.

PEOPLE GENERALLY gave him
what little he asked for,
because he held BIG ENDEARING
IDEAS, that made life
seem spectacular for as long as
a match would burn.
THOSE WHO REMEMBER would say,
'wonder when the KID'S gonna
light another one?'

AFTER A BLACKSMITH welded rear
foot pegs to his 20 INCH FENDERLESS
FRAME... they became pretty much
inseparable – him with that
determined somewhere else look – and
she with a beauty too much for
lessor beings. She'd stand up,
statuesque behind him, hands on
his waist, bending occasionally to
whisper mysteries. She appeared
VISIONS MORE than simply

A GIRL ON HIS BIKE – to anyone
with a pulse – when this little
chariot passed them by.

AN ETERNAL LINGERING THOUGHT
of Cleopatra and the Carnival Kid
consumed whole dinner hours
after THE BIG TENT would
come down upon its week in
each little town; AND TO THIS DAY
Apple Pie America arm wrestles
to say the punch line, 'Well. . .
she was his biggest idea.'

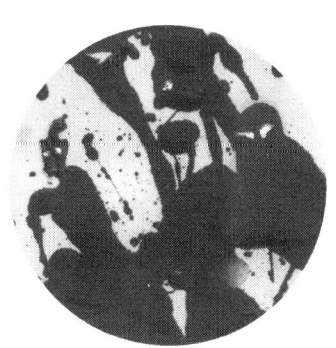

Simply Sunday Claustrophobia

A mashed potato cloud
spit at my window
with bumper crop saliva
and electronic tongue,
as the sports commentator
tried to get excited
about some Babe Ruth-star
sliding to third. . ..
I slap my buzzing ear –
sinister monotony, filled ear,
echoing minister's muttering
broken only by
offering-plate clatter.

Shredded Rice

Coke, cookies, ice cream too,
Smiling faces and hands outstretched,
As they look at me and you.
It seems that this reception dear
Is nothing less than hell.
For while we look bright-eyed and clear,
And very much relaxed,
Our minds are nothing less than taxed
With the thought of leaving here.
So open the presents
And thank the folks,
As they shake and nod their heads.
Some day we will laugh and joke
Of other newly weds.

Observation Dormitory

Sitting here alone,
I wait to hear the phone.
Now it rings so loud and clear
For everyone to hear.
Once then twice, three and four,
Will it ring for evermore?
Each man I know can hear it sing,
And yet he lets it ring.
Why do they not heed the call
Of Peter, John, or Paul?
Perhaps they think, "Oh can't you see,
It's for him, not for me."
Yet on it cries and irritates,
Letting none to concentrate.
By now each man is in a fit,
"Won't someone please just answer it?"
And then from twenty rooms in all,
They dress and stampede the hall.
Now each man runs down the curse,
Heroic efforts about to burst,
Then a chain of voices, "Who's it for?"
And get an answer which deplores,
"That idiot in the twenty first!"

Passing Thoughts

Judgment is the penalty
Which all wise men must pay,
In using rationality,
Observing woeful ways.
Of those I speak are martyrs free,
Who spent their lives in pain.
Indeed they found eternity,
And left a doubtful stain.

Doubtful yes, but not for long
In the course of time,
For weaker minds soon sang the song
With the martyrs lines.
Socrates and Caesar,
Hitler and Macbeth,
Fatalism was their seizure,
Un-natural were their deaths.

Times have changed it must be said,
Our laws have taken care,
Madmen and prophets shed thy blood,
Now they barely get 'the stare.'

Artists and thinkers have their ways,
It is they who plant the sod.
But of such a man they always say,
"God help him, he is odd!"

Please allow me if you will,
To offer some small word,
For I believe there must be still
Some hope for the absurd.

You the fool I do suspect,
Will fall upon your knife.
You will continue to not correct
The follies of your life.

One useless favor may I ask
In your days of zest,
Set aside your pride, your mask,
Don't follow all the rest.

You who are not elite,
Or of any special traction,
The reason for your looking feats
Is merely self-satisfaction.
Do not live by tradition,
Nor leisure on soft pads;

You must seek abolition
Of conformity and your fads.
When you have fulfilled this goal
Not radically, but slow,
Your reason will be like the coal,
our thoughts will brightly glow.

Judgment is the penalty,
Which all wise men must pay,
In using rationality,
Observing woeful ways.

But he who puts his thoughts to good,
Conveyed with wife and brother,
You will be the man you should,
And trod the road much farther.

— 1967

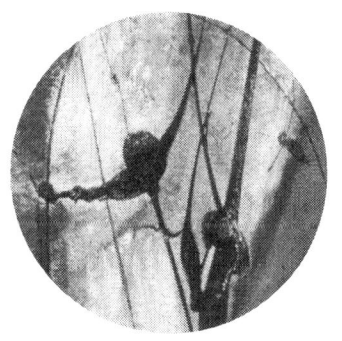

Smoke Chamber

Something about finished brown butts
In a white porcelain tray,
As if to say this rut
Of mine must stop
Before I become the status quo.
Black ashes in their tomb,
Imply there is no room
For health in a stagnant pond
Called life – IF this is life
And living – These substitutes
For pleasure: Then the knife
Be mine – for it has dawned on me
I want out, to get in
A better deal than this. . ..

Star Awards

Every new-spring day
Is a wayfaring search –
Another rung of the ladder –
More eye-ball rolling
and blinking – small talk.
Glowing subtleties will
seldom find compatibility,
for Mr. Homosapien
knows not why beginnings
must have endings.
We are content to drape
our lives with nitty-gritty,
hunky-dory, peanut-butter-jelly.
Concern – How to use it?
We are looking with our hands.

Untitled

We eat our milk
And drink our bread.
Eagle, beagle, squiggle, diggle,
What's wrong with that?

We see through doors
And look out windows.
Pitsy, titsy, witchy, bitchy,
Enjoying our shat.

We kill each other
And starve our brothers.
Fighty, bitey, lovy, dovy,
What's right is right.

It is so very wonderful
To know where we're going.

A Problem

It seems those whom I despise are the boring.
What features make a man worth adoring?
Is it not the self?

By living with a normal,
How can I place dullness
on the shelf,
Yet by living alone,

How can I view the flaws that I wish to dis-own?
Still I am considered drab and plain,

    For I am normal,

    not insane.

Something Else

I speak not of conceit,

        and my heart is not of leather.

                But if you're a stranger and we meet,

                      must we talk about the weather?!!!

The World of Jamie

He's smiling and his lip is curled,
as he hops as and skips and runs.
It seems by being above this world
his happiness has won.
Other times I see his fist
clamped tight with white and rage,
As if it was a train he missed,
or he was locked up in a cage.
Whatever state his mind abides,
he always acts the same;
Not trusting and looking to all sides,
and walks as if he's lame.
While others laugh like elves,
and girls reach for higher limbs,
He quickly reassures himself
for why would they laugh at him?
A private world of bliss and blood
may seem to some a sin;
But me, I wish this insanely flood
would quickly take me in.

— 1967

Untitled

I wish I knew as you well know
Just what there is to knowledge
If I could learn the answer soon
My mind would surely grow.
But while I sit and contemplate
The questions lie before me:
Does knowing mean to master thoughts
Then spend my life reviewing?
Can I learn everything about one thing
Or is this challenge a waste of time in pursuing?
Oh, the thought! – That asking has me knowing
How little I know of what I ask.
All I know is I am confused
About where my thoughts are going.

A Sad Challenge

Loud music fills the air
With every new selection,
As the crowd forgets its cares
And faces no strong new objections.
But amidst these fiery lot . . .
These bloody brains blown sky-high,
One can never fail to spot
That unhappy girl or guy
Who seeks some pleasant atmosphere.
But instead of finding glee,
Only sink more sadly into the beer.
Again I look to the mirror
Which clearly repeats my frown.
So once more I'll walk down
To put my smile against my tears.

Untitled

Lazy-like moans
from the gas grass cutter,
drown in my ear wax,
just as unaware
as the sun's hot arms
that force salty streams
from forehead pores,
slowly down upon
summer-cracked-lips.
A machine and Nature:
both repulsively apathetic –
neither knowing nor caring,
unaware that I prepare
a school year goodbye
to Nancy.

Untitled

"Ladies and Gentlemen,
Our National Anthem."
Then slowly rising,
half apologetically
putting hands on hearts
if his neighbor does,
super American patriots
stumble through words
as difficult to recall
as their Apostle's Creed,
and no longer pretend
to eye the banner
with a pride in its history.

BECAUSE THE NOVELTY
HAS WORN OFF FOR
LIBERTY'S SPOILED
CHILDREN.

Favorite Pronouns

They're meant for each other,
That may be true.
But what do the folks think
Of you, me and you?
You've got what I want
And of me you agree,
So what are we waiting for,
Me, you and me?
You know we can't hurry,
I sure hate to fuss,
But the people do worry
About the two of us.

While It Lasted

A white conglomeration of shapes
made their fall today,
unraveling themselves as a drape
which with the wind did sway
For once, everyone was a grin
playing Indian Poker with their hair,
counting moth balls
behind forehead & chin
of each other's laughing aware.
Covering all frowns,
snow brought us together,
making clowns of solemn persons
now happy to be under the weather.
With snowballs then, the rowdies
got rough,
and Nature's novelty wore off.

Easy Money

Another hard day,
I loosen my collar.
To rake up the hay
And earn the next dollar.
Sweat on my cheeks,
Salt burns these eyes.
My armpits just reek,
I breathe and I sigh.
There's pain in my legs,
I can't wait to sup
As the Devil just begs,
"Please give it up!"
Oh the check may be small
I'm complaining, that's true,
Still I wink to myself
Cause I'm doing it for you.

Happy Outlook

My rusty scent receives the smell
of green grass freshly cut,
And mine eyes do faintly dwell
Upon a squirrel who gathers nuts
In a cute, but cautious manner.
Box cars are locking fast their catches
Out of sight, but sounding off.
A tramp nearby does flick a match
Then spits and loudly coughs.
These gestures see me
above standing still
To glance fully at the view.
With watery eyes, quivering chill,
and a frown.
For without this gripping love from you
I'd still be falling down.

Ode to a Virgin

I laughed with you tonight
as we chased the rain,
pelted by its harmless pain.
Beneath your dripping strands of hair
hid those gay unknowing eyes,
that saw not my disguise.
It was love for which they cared.
But deeper set behind your view
was insight dressed with thoughts,
sensing the truth of those before you.
They have only time to cry
of strangled hearts, tied in knots.
My lust has squeezed them dry.

To David Young

When the folks of elder years
spend their dying days
in search of lost laughs and tears
of youth or moments more gay,
David Young comes to mind.
In his seventies I'm sure,
but roaring laughter, and a sacrilege,
are his mocking cure
against the incidental grays of age
that creep into men of less spirit.
Nothing fragile about David Young:
playing leapfrog from Life,
wagging his whimsical tongue
at non-contender Death.
David Young. He shows the old ladies
that life starts at eighty!

Sharon

You're not here and
the household mirrors
squint to see
what and why
my eyeballs flash about
with the pompous air
of a secret holder,
who wants to let it out
but first to tease awhile.
        Look at me,
           pubic stinky public images,
          and wonder why
your sad boy
suddenly smiles
while chewing gumdrops.
        A god-awful lot
         this town of mirrors
         must be,
         not to know
         the love face
         someone put on me!

Untitled

Brick-building skyscratchers,
sphinxes and tombs,
rooms in the white house,
dark of the moon,
yellowstone park
or paul bunyan's spoon.
Just room for one more –
more than a goose-pimple relic
or stone hauled by
thousands of busted-back men.
Just a hand squeeze,
An honest cheese smile
And she's loving me,
that SHARON – EIGHTH WONDER.

Let love be without dissimulation.

— Romans 13:9

Words of Love

Language from foul lips
Contending with a dog's bark.
A preacher speaks of Noah's Ark,
Men gawk at ladies' hips,
Spectators in the stands,
The foreman's voice,
It's dealers choice,
The cry of swollen glands.
These words of an hour
Change from sweet to sour,
And they bore me,
They do.
Except the three
That do agree,
The three that come from you.

Two Men In Love

It was in the small park
On a late, dim lit day;
My small heart was gay
As the sky fell to darkness.
Two others were there
Walking, hands clutched together;
Just enjoying the weather
Like all lovers in fresh air.
I stopped to pick a posie
While I glanced at their hair:
The same length but who cares,
For I'm just being nosey.
He said "Darling come here,"
Then I ran with much fear
When the same low tone came from her!

Sonnet to Bernie

Was it the first time we met
that our eyes exchanged glances?
They've certainly had their chances
to make a set of us,
But what's your bet?
Yes, you who wears a gay expression
even when the moment
gives your face no precedent for such impressions.
Though our skin may touch,
this day won't find us down the aisle,
no, not for quite awhile.
Still, there is this thought on my tearful cheeks
Maybe years will pass like weeks.

Repellent

Ironically enough,
of all the guys and stuff
in our halls of fame,
we somehow skipped the greatest.
Namely the good citizen
who obeyed the laws, and
for the cause
fought in wars,
and squared the score
with conscientious young objectors;
and who made the 10:30 Service
if Saturday night was not too harsh;
who voted in all elections
for protestant, white, Anglo Saxons;
who ate read meat, beat his wife
only now and then; and
played the great American game
named 'Backseat Congressman.'
The Hall of Fame
awaits you Citizen John Doe,
for you have fulfilled
American ideals
on every count.

The Resolution

It's fall and I'm pooped
Just watching the exhausted trees,
Releasing their heavy burdens
By the twos and threes,
Before the wind blows and scoops
Them into winter mulch.
A personification strikes me dumb
When I become a relinquished twig
Of the apple, peach or plum,
That builds each fruitful crop
Which later dies then drops.
How these determined sticks in the ground
Can hold their arms in the cold,
Waiting for the next revisiting bud,
Is far beyond me!
To this bold patience I adjourn,
In my latest belief
That it's now time to turn-over
A proud, ripe, new leaf.

Prescription

"What is there to success?"
It is only my guess,
But could it be money?
"No friend, it is not!"
Wealthy men have been shot
and those alive are not always gay.
You see, success has a smile,
sometimes for only awhile,
but it is there.
"Then perhaps we can speak
of a solution to seek
with all the right ingredients?"
How about integrity, virtue, and patience true.
Industry and intelligence, through and through.
"Yes, friend, now just add the right companionship
plus the variable of Time,
and you'll be wearing the smile too."

Heartless Switchboard

We were miles apart,
Yet love held us near
To each other's heart.
And when we had thoughts or tears
Or humor to share, we'd call –
By phone – that device that keeps one in touch
With his or her loved one.
Those conversations counted so much.
They were all that was under the sun,
And yet they were bitter:
When we're both at ease,
The words came: "Signal when through, please."
Then we worried about money,
And love was halted by a (CLICK).

Joy in Departing

These seems to be an omen
Designed for those in love,
That makes them dearly covet
Short times spent together.
And if it were not for stamps,
Envelopes, pictures ad long-distance lines.
Time would put the damper
On hateful, happy, and kind exchanges.
Even without these,
Memory would maintain the glee
Of past moments,
Ground into sentiment.
So again history repeats,
As we say goodbye once more.

Untitled

Downtown on a shopping day –
Saturday I think.
What a mirror!
Every reflection the mind's eye
might hope to imagine –
just pushing and scurrying
in a frantic sort of
Social Darwinism,
as I think even the
Salvation Army woman
was trampled to death.
Buffalo herds are almost extinct,
even though they take care of their own.
WHAT'S GOING TO HAPPEN TO US?

Ode to John and Others

Life is full of rude awakenings, tis true,
Which follow not the clock,
For they may come with falling rock,
Or distant day that grows with you.
Oh thank thy lucky constellations
That help you blaze your path;
They've left you not with bitter wrath,
But rather, deep thinking questions and interrogation
Yes, rude awakening lie before thee,
And stare thee boldly in the face;
Ready with a lightning pace
To sweep your mind to sea:
It is there, where you'll go to war.
God pray you meet these awakenings at the shore.

The Mighty Fortress

A small arched frame,
Supports a pious little place
Beneath the steady ticking tapes
Which hold up Wall Street.
A steadfast steeple,
Reminds me that two breeds
Of men – two gods – two types of people
Find their ultimate there.
And you know, that little house of pews
Stands like a rigid rock
Against the rising and falling waves
Of economic interests.
Why is it so damn hard
To kill a church?

Untitled

A close friend's father
was set before
a small local gathering
for final rites.

The man was blessed
with goodness,
and certainly assured
of passing the golden gate.

Yet, damp kerchiefs,
low organ tones,
and somber chorus voices
brought sadness there.

I thought it selfish
We should weep
his premier before heaven.

A Dormant Generation

One escape from life as such,
Exists for all to use.
In fact it's seen so very much,
Perhaps it is abused.

Oh how we long to close our eyes,
During times of need;
To sleep and see the sun arise,
And plant the next day's seed.

When we know tomorrow's fate
To be a throng of joy,
We surely know we can't sleep late,
We'll get up quick, "Oh, boy!"

But if the one that comes real soon
Is apt to be a dread,
We'll swoon into a lengthy dream
Which will keep us long in bed.

Or perhaps it's good just to feel,
When great things have been done,
That we deserve some time to steal;
To relax and not to run.

Well spend your time for what you please,
What err you have at stake;
But I wonder if all sleep would cease,
If man could stay awake.

Untitled

In such a hurry
As they quickly scurry
to soak up the facts
and figures and busy work
involved in an education
And the sex and the booze –
But who's to say what's what.
Quest and question and conquest
and civil rights and riots and
that damn war – they'll take
a stand – any stand cause they
want to find and know.
"god" bless
the college student.
He doesn't know
what's out there for him,
but he's
bustin his mind
to find out.

— 1970

An Ultimatum

That black, bucking bronco
wasn't about to be harassed
or saddled before his time.
His resistance to those
spiteful, spiking spurs
was oath to this. A bit
more of the country side
was his to see, and he'd
give no heed to the placid
life of a spiritless gelding.
Until the last wild mare
was bred, or the sage and
crabgrass gone, he'd just as soon
ream. Do you see the human side to it?

Poop-dee-doo

If I had my way,
I'd have to say,
I sure enjoy the toilet.
But every time I sit my seat,
Someone has to spoil it.
While on the chair,
I'm quite aware,
My business may go bad.
But just to work without the stares,
Would really make me glad.
Surely I have nothing swell,
For anyone to see,
Unless they like the poop, they smell,
Or tinkling of the pee.
Finally the room is clear
Of all those saintly souls,
I am sure that it appears,
There will soon be empty bowels.
Nature calls, all will fall,
A final act in store,
I'm just about to fill my stall,
Then "Oh hell! Who opened the door?"
Well I've given up, It's time to sup,
My time I do abide,
The next time nature calls me up,
I'll have to go outside.

The Folly of Love

To touch a pinecone or smell a plum,
Or taste an egg or lick your thumb.
And to hear the leaves up in the tree,
Without your eyes what good are these?

There is a blindness we must agree,
Involving Tom, Dick, Harry, and me.
We spend our lives hoping and waiting,
Will it come now or while I am skating?
Maybe it will when I'm contemplating.

Suppose we have it after worry and sweat,
And we'll fight to keep it without regret.
Sometimes it's ended at any cost,
All that time, and then it's lost.

This virtue is held high above,
It is charming, yet wretched, for it is love.
An unknown beginning and no small meaning,
It's the one crutch on which we all are leaning.

You hear men say it's a stab in the heart,
"If I had it over, I would never start."
But push it away and claim it a sin,
Man will go right out to find it again!

Untitled

What in the world
Would we ever do
Without some security
With which to fall,
Softly and safely back on

To go without the
bare necessities:
The double garage
a barrage of T.V. sets
And movies twice a week,
The ciggys and the booze.
I know, who's to say
who's to have what?
But ten million people are hungry.

Last Plea of Richard Speck/
Speck's Unanswered Prayer

Forgive me dear God for actions that are inappropriate to the person, time, or place.

Love has dispersed sincerest intentions into a sea of agony, contempt and hatred for all men and women.

I am a derelict that floats upon this aquatic sphere, hoping that my dehydrated soul may once again absorb some healthy thoughts.

My urge to maim or kill is growing as the appetite of an unforgiving parasite.

HELP ME, MR. ALL-KNOWING!

The Gazette

Dow Jones down 5
President goes to Saigon
To sit in the Sun.
Crime Rate rapidly increasing
Riots spread to TEASING KANSAS.
Congress debating
Foreign policy.
Poverty program tabled.
Extra!

TROLLS go on strike for Food,
Claiming they will starve
If America keeps saying
"We'll put that bridge off
until we come to it."
America, stop crossing oceans
and start crossing bridges!

Untitled

Millions for defense
and not one cent for tribute.
Where did I hear that before?
It must have gone
to someone's head,
as it now stands
"Billions for defense
and aggression, but not
one cent for bread."
Oh well, I have faith
in this American Government
of ours – they know what's best.
They must, because
a few hundred thousand
guys lie still, and ten million
folks are very hungry.
      JUST HAVE FAITH!

Untitled

"Fee, Fie Fo Fum,
I smell the blood of an Englishman,
a Frenchman, a Russian,
a German, a China man,"
said the giant.
"I am America the great,
the powerful, the defiant.
Who but me has influence
from ocean to sea?
Who but me can have
my hands in the
affairs of other lands
when my policies
are in a state of political sham?"
    THE ROMAN EMPIRE?

Melting Testimony

Floating, gliding, slowly I Fall,
My crystal structure bright;
With a body large or small,
I come at day or night.
A flake of ice, I am known,
White, light, fragile and froze.
In still or wind, I am blown
And fall to earth or someone's nose.
Of all the states that nature owns,
Like rain or breeze or sun,
More songs and indeed more poems
Talk of me, I'm the one.
But what about my destiny,
Am I prone to doom?
Or will my life be filled with glee,
To know for me there's room?
No my flake, you must die,
The will of God is felt.
Before you tell them God is nigh,
Your body will be melt.
Yes my flake, you've seen His light,
You've felt His warming love.
But proof of Him we hold so tight,
They need faith in Him above.

Untitled

A slick-stepping memorial band
made its known in our dining room,
led by the grand-old flag
and an inspirational drum.

Like a rag of grease and grime
which was bought at five and dime,
our banner caught less respect
than those who carried it.

Out marched the singing patriots
being awarded a standing ovation
by those with reservations
about doing such a thing.

For everyone knows that American heritage
is the rust of antiquity.

Downpour

It's rained and poured for days,
And continued through the nights.
I cannot see the sun's rays,
I cannot see the bright lights.
Not rain, not rain tis true,
The facts I won't construe;
It's tears that wet my sky,
And these painful tears won't dry.
What's the forecast of tomorrow,
Is it joy or is it sorrow?
Only time will tell.
But my heart cannot vacation
In this precipitation,
Until these eyes get well.

Optimism

You ask me each day
As we stop on the way,
Just what it is that
I am thinking.
For no matter the season,
You wonder the reason
Which keeps my red eyes
From their blinking.
And each time I turn,
So you won't learn
About the big tears
That I'm hiding.
Yes I'll hang tough,
Though it is rough,
To smile again
Time abiding.

2

Towards Life in General

MY TWO BEST answers for,
"Why do YOU write poetry?"

Because I have to. I really must.

Because I hope to expand reality.

Down in the Mouth

The Pope is priming Poland,
the Duke is in LaDuke.
The President is impressing,
the King is dining kings.
Johnny Cash is in his element,
for some this life is fine,
but Billy Boy lost his luck,
he's sucking on his wine.

The Annuity
(for Rocky)

Palette shades of Life
beginning freshly made
emotions within my
child, my child;
a dog, a bicycle, a communion,
first glimpses of what is to come,
followed by another, and another;
through all the subtle human hues
of things undone and things we do,
I've come to love one more time
new things of you,
my brother, my brother.

— March 22, 2017

The Big

A larva chigger
chiggered me,
it jumped my skin
from its tree,
along the walls of river rock,
where Chulo Canyon's vista locks
Coronado's Keyhole.

Though its
fluid poisons me,
I do not take it personally.
I too evolve
in this place, where
egg sacs spawn
the mighty mite.

Thirty days leave
from humming birds
and talking streams,
I scratch my wounds in retrospect,
triggering the chiggering
of high desert's scheme,
a bit of me included...

— October 2010
Revised November 2012

The Big

A larva, chigger
chiggered me
it jumped my skin
from its tree,
along the walls of river rock,
where Chulo Canyon's vista locks
Coronado's keyhole.

And while its
fluid poisons me
I do not take it personally.
I too evolve
in this place where
larva spawns
the mighty mite.

Thirty days leave
from humming birds
and talking springs,
I scratch my wounds in retrospect
triggering the chiggering
of Chulo Canyon's scheme of things,
a bit of me included.

Something Said, Something Done

We fell into a triangle,
a foursome if you count
the dog. Effortless, our union
led us by increments.
Its origins we noisily summarized,
carrying on...
We began our easy breezy serendipity,
built upon something done,
something said.

We made euphoric plans; carefully wrapped
outings gingerly carried in woven baskets.
When it felt safe, we edged into unsafe places,
jangling irreplaceable keys
as if they no longer mattered,
making ourselves vulnerable,
not noticing that in the mix
there came a thief.

Suddenly our precious
alliance went missing,
taken into the great unseen,
and completely disappeared.
I, robbed, could not retrace
which leaf had killed our Tree;
only that an extended, stunning
silence now fell upon me.

Not wanting to leave the crannies
where voices used to be,
I shuffle, detecting
the faint, colorless residue of
friendship, imagining perhaps
a ghost barely residing, of
something said,
something done.

— September 1, 2014

The Colonials

Somehow,
masthead ships
with wooden lips
kissed goodbye to minarets
and obelisks, tablets, scrolls,
sarcophagus and gutty words
with I's and Q's
for something new, somehow.

New Nation place
in Appa-shena-blue-ridge world,
they flipped the hull
on grassy yarn,
called the thing
Virginia Barn,
and began cohabitation.

Alice, Suzie, Summer, Robin,
Nicholas rides old Spartacus
while Alwyn signals Jasper.
Ditzie warms the
wise one's lap,
Phoenix takes another nap,
Mooshoo judges from aloof,
Frankie paces on the roof,
Barbara's jesting, she's the goof,
and Loki's running faster.

No standard deviation
within this pastoral proposition.
No pyramid precise,
no Spanish Inquisition
among these free speech makers,
gleefully dancing to their Yodalodials.
They are parents, scrappers,
resourceful muckrakers to the end,
perfecting wisdom by starting again,
where the winding road comes to a bend,
three days with the Colonials.

— December 2009

Nineteen Fire Fighters Dead

A week of high desert
summer swelt,
unable to focus,
shoe leather sticking
to asphalt melt,
no need to answer types
asking, but only after three
whiskeys and a water belt,
"Every year the monsoons
get here late – why,
why so late?"
Just when the usual pitifulness
of the man altering weather debate
turned muted and soluble – a distant
lighting crack, a foreboding roll
of timpani drums, grew into
violent sounds like missiles attacking
a continent of ice.
Morphing then, Nature's fire
breathing dragons prepared to
descend over a canyon
of kindling, scorched earth,
and dread.

— July 2013

Short Story

He was jaded, cold, assuming.
You were not.
In the cocktail fumes
of social cool – you reached,
still an innocent,
turning to tell
all the truths of us – and
when I saw what you were doing,
I bowed as the two of you
went away, scarcely surprised
that you just changed reality
for the three of us.

— 2011

Bad and Bad

I killed someone.
Someone killed me.
He went bullet limp,
an intruder in my lover's nest.
I followed slowly,
digesting a slug,
stopping long enough
to reckon with its steady funneling
drain of life's ingredients,
into an unknown container
filling up with my vibrant death.

Bad timing and rape,
the Bad Man's legacy.
Mine a gratuity of
final thoughts,
an unnatural reconcile full of
sincere goodbyes,
grateful that dying took awhile,
long enough to see that
I killed someone.
Someone killed me.

— June 2013

Living Out Loud

Living out loud,
Having clear intentions,
into the nothing
looking for the something,
without looking back.

Hearing song
streaming in thought,
aware, mindful, too alive to
go quietly, uneventfully
at death's punctuation.

Peering between
the past and death's shadow,
two vast nothings, hoping to
maintain composure:
"What is this, exactly,
and Why does it exist?"

— February 12, 2013

Red Limerick

Rouge Rock, Sedona and the Stars,
Dyanna and Val run the Bar,
Martini and Cosmo do Sashay,
when Top Cuisine shouts "Cache!"
It's Chef Ron's time to lead the way.

— June 27, 2012

Girl on the Ruins

Where human sacrifice and gold
flooded these steps of Mitla,
bringing only the disappointing
conquistador gods and disease...
you sat.

Nearly a falcon's distance away,
still I made you out as distant,
tall, svelte, fair skin angled
in your thatched hat,
warding off the sweltering hater of Europeans.

I watched you from this bird's eye,
seeing you alone, comfortable, unaware
of the height, down your long feet
on short Mayan treads, making me wonder
whether you too were on the ruins.

— 2008

Gun

"When the 'Bad Man' comes,"
I used to say,
bombarded like everyone else
with the math of bloody evil events,
reported graphically and
gratuitously in the murky malaise
of our risky microcosm.
Until one day I went to the store
and bought a tool; and I learned
how to use it.

Then I waited...
for whatever bugaboo
intended to cast a fate upon me.
Unlike other utensils
this one moved with me
from room to room.
It waited patiently for me
under mattress and cushion,
in drawers and beneath
car seats, staying close
as any deep secreted friend.

I became mindful,
aware of my compadre at the ready,
it never whined,
nor needed food, nor betrayed
what we enjoyed together.
The more companion trips
we made to remote places
testing its reliability – the more
my sidekick became an animated 'Who.'

I named it 'Prudent," cleaning it,
handling it, acknowledging it.
I do not remember ever talking to
my new abettor, or saying "good night."
But we had something special, and
I became changed in a measurable way,
more assured and willing to
wander without my loyal trustee.
But that is not to say
I hold my Prudent in
any less regard,
my solace, my confidante, my gun.

— November 10, 2012

Sedona Haiku #Spring

White water creek running

the sound drowning highway noise drones

gurgling past the carved,

un-cunning.

Girl on the Ruins II

When you
laid finally on your hand-me-down,
wondering whether
all your disappointments
were real, as you
became the girl
every man wanted,
the muse of every love song,
every heart's simple tune,
every dream dreamed
by every princess,
and yet...
no longer the innocent being led
up the pyramid steps,
not the girl on the ruins.

— May 2011

Domestic Dispute

A blue ribbon pair
from Mount Sibble,
kept marital spats
to a dribble.
When asked of their guide
to Love's exceptional ride,
"More Sex!" he clamored.
"Less Quibble," she replied.

— May 2013

Repercussions

You are the Tide,
cradling all
in your tubular twirl,
dropping sea creatures
stop by stop.
Your moon tables are
fixed and affirmed.
You do what you do,
your return route not swayed
by dodders delayed,
powering back without them.
Not a debate.
No rebuttal.
You are the Tide.

— February 8, 2013

Class of '66

Back then the
prairie wind took a breath
and blew us in.
"What are your fears,
and who are your friends?
Wanna do something, later?"

Now. . . it's later. Much later.
"Is it still you? What'd ya find?
Did you love?
Come closer. What do you see?
Tell the truth. Look what time
has done with me?"

A mixer, a tour,
a moment of silence
for the fallen, a memorial
for the brave. Pondering
the life we started and
the lives we've made.

Then. . . we scattered
and scouted with the wind again,
riding away on our roundabouts.
What did we learn?
Lots. Nothing. Life is weird.
School's never out.

— July 2, 2016

The Highness

. . . of it all. Yes, more human
acts of mutual exploitation are possible;
like this – your female folds
and my muscle,
shall never be remiss
as long as we ball into our tangle.

You get it, I know – the adding,
the multiplying – the exponential
quality of kisses – OUR kisses – our
wet wishes of lust and love's dishes.
Simplicity, enormity, even guano and scat,
continuous, messy, piled high –
what's wrong with that?

Out

It is late in the day
and I am unwarmable,
my feet having become
wooden blocks against obligation.
A light dust is gathering
upon me in the motionless.
My mind defiant,
detaches, fixed into
its own final looking out.
The birds dig deeper
for seeds muddied down,
not withered by any
waning fizz of clichés.
It is late in the day of unfeeling,
as the "I" runs out of
mood to face the opposition.

Stop, Look, Listen

The affable looking man tore his bread
into thumbnail sized sponges,
dabbing, soaking up au jus,
then wrapping them around
even smaller pieces of chunk food.

— Sedona, AZ, 2012

More Than One Mantra II
(this one is mine)

Integrity
Honesty
Discipline
Hustle
Humanity

Chesney

"People like me,"
that's what you said.
"If something in my
life were broken, I'd
fix it," that's what you said.

When dues paying
members know that
a man has figured out
the truth, that man is King.

Good thing, too.
I've been in a corner
and it helped to ask,
"What would Chesney do?"

— February 20, 1996)

Plutocracy

Massmatically inclined
sizemographers excised
the "Loveable Little One'
from children's book lopapalooza,
like we would never notice.

As if we
did not already know
that when it comes to
things that matter…
only a few get to vote.

(upon removal of Pluto from the
Planetary System)

Perfect Saint

Any words
used to illuminate a saint
are borrowed from the worthy.
I am not.
I am the skin of every human act
that needs forgiving.
Even I have felt the light of Teresa.
She, Teresa, to the poorest of poor,
at home in her own poverty.
So why did you make her
wait so long? How many millions
more could she have lifted in her death
without your required proofs,
your ceremonious sanctity?
Let Teresa be the final saint,
the perfect saint. Let Teresa
work unfettered by forms and
testimonials, for god's sake.
Let Teresa tend to the destitute dying
as I the wretched, willingly wait
only in need of mercy, undeserved.
In this we are all poor.

— September 4, 2016

Dying Destitute
(for Mother Teresa)

The only sign of life
in the poor pencil-legged thing
with the holocaust eyes – came as
a struggling ooze of pus.

Still, the scowling wealth grubbers
rained their industrious excrement
upon this dying destitute.

For not striving toward a better future;
for the living dead man's alms begging;
for his membership in the cult of suffering.

But this was the 'Year of Mercy,'
with a powerful new saint
tending to his maggots.

By which she caused the money lords
to look away in shame for the crime of
poverty, which they created.
And that became the Third Miracle.

— September 4, 2016

Piece of a Prayer

We ask you to revenge
our unhealing wounds;
we do not want to
know what you do
when no one is looking.

To us, you are
the considerate, deliberate,
dangerous kind;
our young sisters
wanted to be with you.
Our childish limerick jests,
discerning yes, but
did you really care?

Years of drinks later,
so many losing bets;
we still ask you, tearfully,
our expectant hope rising,
to win for us.
For the eternal time
you sigh,
"Truth? Or Dare?"

— Late July 2013

Life Part I
The Last Act

When I pause
from mundane things,
the bell for lonely people rings,
we lonely know what it means,
this fading tone of people cheer,
the sounds of when we
held them near, then
drove them off, tear by tear,
parading our ferocity
in this proud life we chose,
we the bellicose,
screeching to be lonely.

Life Part II
Purgatory

Occasionally we meet by fire,
anger, self-loathing, out desire,
therapy the sum of
our decline, rotting teeth,
breasts resigned,
don't pray for us,
we saw this coming.
Bullets, knives, irks and ires,
standing by what we have sired,
livers, kidneys, hearts have burst,
cannot be healed,
we can't be nursed,
could hell be worse?
could hell be worse?

Life Part III
Heaven – Or Is It?

No I.
No why.
No no.
No yes.
Life's efforts no longer missed,
gone through that to get to this.
Still, I see you there
where I atoned, I see
the way you cry alone.
Feeling I am sent back
on the words of an angel's trust,
"You must, sinner, sorry...YOU MUST!"

Higher Limit

There is one player
at the table I cannot beat.
Eight men falling upon
their tells and tell-tells indiscreet.

He and I measure each other
hand for hand – darting, stabbing,
slogging, he jabs at my chips,
his collectibles.

Somehow he reads my glances,
tics, detectable – from what
magic lens I do not know.
Chinks in my armor have begun to show.

Then, when our wager stacks collide
in a maelstrom of why-oh-whys...
EVERYTHING about us at stake
in one final eye-to-eye...
I retreat again, still 'alive,' but
feeling worthless deep in the gut of poker.

— 2010
(revised 2012)

Felton Elton Singing Under the Nails of the Strawberry Blond
(bar napkin #172)

On the night of a
full moon we
race across the desert plain,
the lights turned off;
the saguaros dance
with the willowy spoons;
unidentifiable silhouettes
run wild on this wilding night;
nights like these,
one's entire universe
hinged upon the weensy,
where one man, one soul
amongst billions by
saying "Yes!" can grab
the whole thing and
skip it across God's hand.
See what you made me do?
And none too soon.

— 1987

Felton Elton Singing
Cinful her Rails my berry
~~Bu~~ the Strawberry
Blvd
#172

On the night of the
full moon I
raced across the desert
plain the lights burned at
the Suazo's cabin
with the desert spare
~~they~~ the silhouettes running
wild on the wildest night
these things hinge on
the universe
~~see to keep that~~
~~also that~~ nothing mystical

Bots

Robots
Throwbots,
and Bots to change
your bed;

Warbots
Thorbots,
filling enemies
with lead;

Words not
Love not,
obsoletes in
dusty sheds;

"Never thought
it would come to naught,"
the last thing
ever said.

Advice

Get social media
felt like get disgust.
To become a loathsome atom,
all the village warned,
"Shed your phobia
for our utopia,
you absolutely must!"
So I pondered every key stroke,
to join the human race,
I tapped on 'Enter, Control, Escape,'
Now... I'm trapped in cyberspace.

— June 2017

Birthday Girl Limerick

A Fred Astaire
dancer named Flo,
taught the birds to dance long ago;
the jays do the salsa,
the cardinals the waltz,
and Flo is the star of the show.

Town

The piano player
is pounding.

The know-it-all
is expounding.

I shall leave you
as the words left me.

— 1989

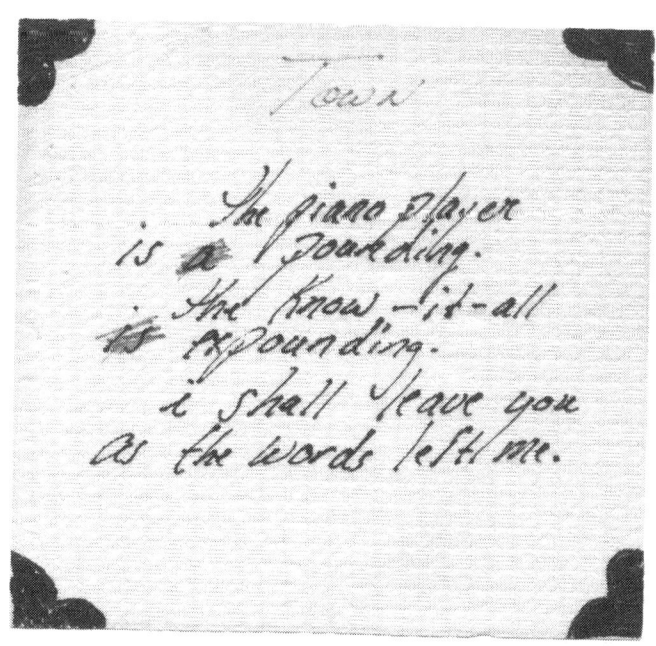

The Ribbon Cutters

It was a spiffy
neighborhood and we
looked out for each other –
open houses and block parties
occurring with the best intentions,
there on the green tree-lined streets
and cul-de-sacs. We were pleasant,
potluck, mid-sized car people, who
'brought out own.'
One night, new neighbors
made a 'to do' about some newsy
thing – the body count imbalance
in Gaza. They provoked. They pressed
for individual opinions, these nice new people
put the whole party into a frazzle, when finally
the host that night simmered these real troopers
by asking, "How do you want your steaks?"
Calm restored, someone thought
to raise a toast, "To the Pragmatic Generation."

— July 29, 2014

The Icon

The excavators'
stockpiled materials
got re-arranged to shape
a grand restaurant, a Taj of
polished slates and metals
tall enough to realize a shadow,
whose fingers cooled the air for
ravens, and further drew the eye
to a famed mountain scape.

One day I stood on a walkway
across the street from this new icon,
wanting to better appreciate the majesty
of minds, and money, and the hundred thousand
parts that the foreman assembled before we could eat.
"What is it?" each passing stranger asked, each halting
to see what I was seeing. "Oh my," I sang like a
park ranger on tilt, as if each passerby should
already know so worthwhile a thing,
"That's the place that Jac Robson built!"

Depression

Listen to the wind and rain
In the deep and heartless black,
That brings to bear all the pain,
And takes my mind far back
To days when the sun shone sharp
Upon the glow of my virgin youth.
The mother from whose womb I barged
Must have sensed my fate.
For now she cries with tears enlarged,
Because her womb I hate.
By what cause did she bring
Another hungry mind,
Which she surely knew would cling
To infamy-temptation-pride-mankind?
These are the detestable thoughts
Which drive my mind to dust,
And incite the doubts which have been wrought
As to my existence, is it just?
Remember those sacred, precious days
When the sun shone right,
Reflecting itself in contented ways,
Then guarding them through the night;
When the dawn was worth waiting for,
Until the dusk came into sight?
Every moment was shared with HIM,
Never was I alone,
His divinely rays tanned my skin,
Painting me in confidant tones.

Now, all pivots from yellow,
That virtue which knows no slack,
Towards vicious pleasures mellow,
And quickly turning black.
No more longing to learn,
I live without cares;
Towards others no concern,
With them nothing to share.
"What is a dream?" I ask the past.
"Is it for the untarnished who look ahead,
Hoping for love, their stable mast,
Then only to be blown back instead?
Or is it for the old and despaired,
A fantasy of escape,
For the sentimental life which they once cared,
Then by nature of reason was raped?"
Oh you senile detestable vaults,
Your dark rationalizations seek to cover
All your pride and all our faults
By music, speech, lies, or lover.
No, Darkness, you'll not claim this life
With worry and reason, my god faith
Strengthens me in trouble and strife.
For man is not a rational being,
And has no grounds for rational thought.
This will be seen,
His time is not earned and easily bought.
Most despised of him is said,

The statement used, "At last."
If only he'd not fear the dead,
And shut away the past,
With gleaming eyes to see the 'morrow.
Take now this lever
To pry away fermenting sorrow,
Moving forward ever, backward never.
Forgive me now, for in my pity
All I've done is swim.
And in my own collective city,
Is just another whim.
And yet somehow it seems so real,
As my wakened mind looks back,
That someone did my yellow steal,
And colored it all black.

3

For Love and Lovers

Music and laughter every day,
Loyalty in the face of doubt, torment,
torture and even death.
Every moment together or apart,
has the ingredients of foreplay.

To have a friend you gotta be a friend.
To get a letter, you need to write a letter.

To find Love...

Love's Affirmation

"I am always me when I am thinking of You."

First Love Note to My Mother
(Age 5)

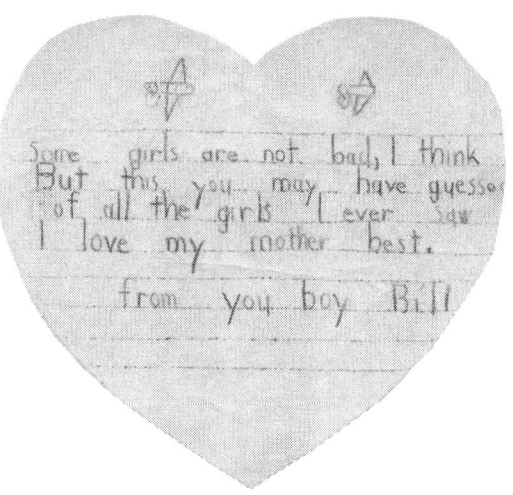

Some girls are not bad, I think.
But this you may have guessed,
   of all the girls I ever saw,
     I love my mother best.

   from your boy Bill

— 1953

K.G.B.

Dressed in alchemist's gown,
thinking he could put a
recall on Earth's most elegant idea.
Dredging up in his mindful net,
tugging up on down under things,
a gooey sweat on every
bell that rings,
the sound of love on everything,
sounds like I, like you, like they,
like we, as he reveals himself
to Kimberly G.

Char

Thinking of the warmth
and the giving of it
which you bestow unto me;

Thinking of those eyes
god gave you
And the many poses they can make;

Thinking of you quivering
after the unrobing,
And then the intake of
the length of me;

So the fact remains
that we are wed
In the spirit of creating
substance in one another;

And the Love is in the
Giving;
And the Eternity is in the
Loving Memory –
and We are both of these.

True Story

Child of the Albatross
by your own guile wit
this bus ride will never
cease. I must know if
there really is a Venus,
indeed I'll be
on time, but the lonely
hurt of tired lights unwelcomed
bids a "travel on, driver,
travel on."

Luminous, nocturne, centerlines
blur, your city falls back,
sinking like a junkie's friendship
lulled away in the drone engine
snuggled to the ear.
So you think you'll
know me still where we
collide a year from now?

Taste again!
my pollen is a
poltergeist – look up
lonely analytical child
a falling star in Orion's
soup, coachman and his
coachery fading out of focus,
immune to your daggered daisies,
a rousing voice
muffled by the tinted glass,
"travel on, driver, travel on."

— January 1975

Estranged

Somewhat unnatural of course,
was this deep-rooted view
over all things visible to
my mind's eye, as I
addressed knowledge with blissful remorse
and cried, "I love you."
To be in love with understanding,
and wonder whether we were compatible!
Conquered, I long for the abstract
unfathomable and not within grasp.
Blessed am I, for this longing
to learn n'wil let me tire –
it will ne'er let me aspire
to any but it – TRUE LOVE.

We Never

Didn't know you
you didn't know me.
Two acts of kindness
for every low blow.
The wind used to howl
outside our window,
hurricanes on the moon,
white camps trim the sea.
Woman you are too close
to my danger, can't you see?
Panther on the roof top
exuding his slow stride.
I'm breathing hard inside of him,
my ferocity untied.
"It's just a cat, silly," your own
jaded breath subsides.
And like that I saw the future
of our intimacies du jour.
"We'll never fall in love," I mused,
"and that I know for sure."

— 1981

Sexus

Masculine – Feminine,
feline – growl,
svelte, melt, pelt, belt,
spirit on the prowl;
jagged, jaded, goofy, gore,
as it has been evermore.

Fierce and tall
before the fall. I met You.
Little French poodles mowing their lawns,
hair drying the morning dew,
our little life in tidy string bows,
what a way to go.

—— 1984

Chiracahua

On a short winter day,
the cabin fire
sent me for more wood.
A snow drift in the scrub
oak trees delayed me
just long enough to see
fresh tracks fading
on the Apache Trail.
A bobcat? A bear?
No. The feet of a woman,
I became more aware,
sensing her stop just ahead
to measure my threat,
animal eyes about to meet
in a way that colors out everything
in survival's palette,
suddenly, no other way it could be.
As solitary animals, I knew of her
and she knew of me,
the loneliest of animals
sharing a moment
in the we... we... we...

— November 1985

Akasha

Fate painted us
with pompous jest,
a man tortured
by his perdu,
confined now with a woman
whose name was Verity.
Two strangers hooked
in an airport moment,
each longing to hide
a secret in the other, as an offering
to someone you never thought
you'd ever meet, holding something you
never thought you'd tell.
Then it happened, and it was not a game.
Asked. And answered,
as if by a soothsayer's spell,
"I will never lie,
if You will tell the truth."

— December 1992

Love Subtle

It seemed
nothing more than
a working day,
an hour's work
for an hour's pay.
Never reaching the summit
of the paper mountain shuffle,
the heavy weight
of time passing,
grew... and grew... and grew,
unable to find meaning
in anything I would do.
Then... a song bird sang
in a meadow somewhere.
A sweet flooding sound
that began as a pure droplet
of morning dew,
rushed over the trivia
the better to find you.
From here it provides
Love's view.
Changed, I wake up
each morning asking,
"Did you feel it too?"

— June 2002

Alana Marie Davis

Thank you for laughing!
Thank you for caring,
for daring to be YOU at the
same time in the same place
with me, in the uncertainty of
being natural, while breathing in...
and breathing out.
You are fearless
to host a hedonist,
a foggy soul,
a killer in your Holy Place,
feeding me, wiping my tearful eye,
while I stay to slay evil outside,
in your disappearing universe...

— 2007

EK II

You knew
You'd never be
True blue,
Didn't you.

Love Then and Now

For once love was no fantasy,
no social chatter
dependent upon looking
back, our love felt
no need to reminisce.
Our rime together
exhilarated in its ride.
Even when we
let love do the driving
it kept us alive,
no near misses,
nothing to halt the mountains,
the rivers,
the flowers
from blowing us kisses.
For once love was allowed
to be here now,
love allowed to linger
wherever we are.
Spoonful by spoon
I see you, real, illuminated
in few words.
You are not moonstruck.
You shoot the moon.
We're no star gazers.
We ride the stars.

— March 2007

The Secret

Her darker side.
A deep, deep need
to be erotically controlled,
something primordial
I supposed, hidden and
aching in the soul.
Bushes stirred,
an animal smelling
the animal in her,
filling the far reaches,
leaving no empty holes.
Nothing like it,
nothing understood.
She did not try to explain,
even if she could,
keeping her pleasure warmed
in the safe of a
dangerous itching inquiry,
"What else do you know about me?"

— August 2007

About Shelly Bean

She stayed with me
all night and waking,
selfless in spite of me,
a gift of the sincerest kind.
I relived a life of torrid tales
while she lovingly held the lamp,
my nightingale.

— February 2008

Predisposed

Something we said in unison
at the start, something laughable,
"Love only happens when we're apart!"
Each separation longer
as if we were obligated
to respect an invisible
pact, suggesting the blank spaces
made us more romantic,
more poetic, more alive.
When holding hands
became silently accusatory
of feelings contrived,
we sunk lower,
looking for signs.
Then... two doves nesting in
a high rise escaped a falcon,
falling safely towards us
down on the street,
and one of us said "oh how
sweet!" And then and there
our love, our lonely love
became very faint and
so discreet, as a ghost love,
our lonely elusive love.

— April 2011

Wrought

"How shall it come?"
we ask now with
metric assurances
about the yawning, bitter End.
The steady warming,
the quickenings of self-destruction,
the pestilence and pandemics
arriving in narrower gaps.
These unforgiving virulent strains
and tipping points, churning
waning Earth into morbidly elegant
evenness, our once compelling rhetoric
blended into the undertow of a
dreary pudding, wrought by hand,
by willfulness,
by indifference.

Having acquiesced, OUR LOVE
undisturbed, unbinds itself joyously
to create our own master plan
for the Final Event. We dance daily
under the sentencing that lives
quietly, bitterly, overhead and
alone in each mind,
the unspoken angst
of our dissolving mankind.
How free it feels!
Preparing to bid Earth adieu,
choosing the best part of it,
the End of the World
together with You.

— January 7, 2012

Ions

Blurring through space as children,
blank uncertain,
indiscriminate – and unaware
that we were drawing like static
towards each other. Then. . . a fully charged
moment and my oath
to never let a spider get you.

It was a good night for it, with
so many stars to choose from,
each patiently holding its
dazzling pageant, waiting to be plucked.
You carried yours without damage
into your dreams. Mine lit up a saddle bag
as I made my way home along Chimney Rock.

Impossible not to wonder as I went. . .
with all that fabled light, soft, lip-jumped
into the cataclysmic kaplooey,
and still carrying my own glow. . .
did we change an outcome
by being in the same place
at the same time?

— Revised 2012

Jaci Land

It could just as
easily have been the other
way around;
the way around 'what ifs' and
'why didn't I's' and the
nightly lurches of a man slowly drowning.

She decided
otherwise, choosing to see
hearts;
and when she shooed away the last
shadow of death, distant drums
of change arrived...

...as a marching band. They carried
her about with the likes of Queen Da Vina,
Dixie Diva, Katie Lady, and Coyote Cal;
they exuberated!
And it was
no time to be unhappy.

— January 22, 2012

For Jaci

We do not work
at our love.
Millions toil
to provide a
wage so worrisome,
life surely shortened
by its broad laboring strokes,
given to moving and
dividing as we are
consigned to do.
My love and I
do not work
at the utterly and
the everything, the all and
the nothing more
than a word, a gesture,
the easy breeze of
man apart from himself.
My Love and I
do not weary over miracles,
nor subtle gifts.
We do not work.

— February 2012

The Wilson

Dixie Diva
saw dogs in the clouds:
a schnauzer, toy poodles,
some dobies – even a cow!
Our over active minds
whimseyed in this lollygangaroo,
(and I got to be a dreaming dog too).
You should have been there.
We named a cloud after you.

— March 2012

Nocturne in Love Flat Lately
(for Jaci)

Our Love...
came into view
long and lovely.

It sang for us,
of Red Bird
outside lately.

Then you knew from
your own crested doo,
how serenades chisel
and sand, so sedately.

How long will we exist?
What do we have, and
what is this?

Red Bird's sweet whistle,
his wooing epistle
decrees hearts to abide.
It is for Love to happen,
not to decide...

— March 10, 2012

Quixotic

You paused, then turned
only slightly from your pleasant way.
Love's naysayers scoff and muse
that you may have lost
only an eyelash.
I saw more – a Torah Scroll
dropped, an inconceivably small speck
of your willful hinge vaporized,
passing silently, invisibly, through the air.

The planet our love lives on
lilted only so, but with such consequence.
Atone! Life don't be cheap,
and murky, and so much a liar!
Not to worry, Love,
my butterfly net, my magic word
and I ride shouting after you.
"ZERBO!"

— May 12, 2012

Over Jaci's Shoulder

Sun came through the window
a certain way,
and you said, "don't let it sway you."
Do you remember
laying on your side,
posing botticellian without posing?
Do you?

Before that a curtain of rain
parted, exposing our rouse,
fuming the place with its
April morning mulchy mist.
Do you remember its alchemy
of red desert mud and musk, teasing out
a purring giggle? Do you?

Before, During, and After.
A butterfly came briefly in,
sticking to, tickling you with
its curious mouth over your kissy dew.
And you who I'd never seen giggle,
giggled again. Do you remember?
Do You?

We mooshed together
In a body toast about "Never Forgetting,"
as we rose and ironed smooth
our rumples with civility. Do you remember
glancing over your shoulder briefly, as the
really big something digitized away?
Do you?

— April 10, 2012

Jaci in the Night

Something said
stepped on our love,
wedging us in two
where once we were one.
Something said
more than something done,
snapping us like
a droughted twig,
calling quickly now
everything into question.
Who could not marvel that
our monument – the fabled
tower of considerations,
carefully fitted kiss by kiss
could be toppled, now unkissed,
imploding like this,
bringing us down to our dust.
Then... you retraced tears
to our sacred place... standing
at first, still angry in
your offering of lace
until I, too, calmed and cooed,
drying your face.

Who could not exalt
how lively we returned
to Love's Body,
all that was acid
now is glue,
then arguing playfully about
where birds go at night,
and about who saved us,
was it me, or
was it you?

     — May 30, 2012

Angelina Jolie

Nobody asked me.
"The most beautiful woman
in the world" – that's
what they declared.
Could they possibly
have met and judged
all the others?
To have overlooked
your enduring lips,
your gliding hips,
your klieg light eyes granting
safe passage thru nightly skies –
skews this thing so not right.
Nobody asked me.
They do not feel and
see your warm loaves seal
with dreamy folds,
your exotic streams exhaled,
bringing all nocturnal ships that sail,
to easy shore by morning.
If a moniker mere gadflies
seek to ring loud about
this fantasy thing – then
I now name YOU to be,
the more perfect Angelina Jolie.

— June 11, 2012

Big Moon in the Dragoons

"You Are Invited,"
the message said,
a whispered breeze
inside my head,
come dance and free
to desert tunes,
where stony glens
store god's Dragoons,
"and bring your True Love with you."

Unevenly balanced oblongs
of many tons,
giant egg stacks
greeted us, monumental
one-by-one.
Shadows looming inexact
to our delight,
greeting throngs in lunar light.

Gila Monster swung Monitor Liz.
Thirsty creatures in grassy bibs
sucked from straws a milky jizz,
flowing through Agave's ribs.
Vistas viewed from Saguaro's arms
while first we imbued Elixir's song.
Barrel's jig exuded charm,
not a soul dared to cop a yawn,
predators – now disarmed.

Then... True Love
waltzed with Mountain Lion,
Puma Bear kept on trying,
where Geronimo,
where Victorio lay
disguised as scorpions,
their stingers swayed,
we polka'd and tango'd
to the "hey, hey, hey!"

Gypsy moths
strobed their wings,
Buzzy Fly and Cicada
did rhythmic things,
Apache drums woke Cochise Stronghold King,
Dung Beetle and Stink Bug chums,
twirled the rings off Corral Snake,
to a bevy of warblers doing
one more take.

Time lapsed,
frame by frame,
on lupine moss
our wildings tamed,
Pack Rat boss pilfered
a caviar spoon
for flat bread and cactus jam,
we divvy now our bits of swoon,
and Moon eclipsed goes on the lam...

Hitch-hiking Comet's tail
and gaining time,

we compose OUR tale,
g-forced back to nursery rhymes.
"And you landed in a butter cup?!"
As former children
now resigned,
"we made it up.
We made the whole thing up!"

— June 19, 2012

Two Toasts for Jaci

PATIENCE...

She's my muse.
If it be magic
she lives in me,
where beautiful words
seem to be
waiting. We cross deep fiords.
She helps me find jewels
in life's rubble as we climb,
"Patience, Polite, Plenty of Time.
.."

HOW FAR...

Twilight
rearranges what Day has done;
Mountain Shadows
softly stirred
and gently steeped,
the last thought each Night
I try to keep,
"How far Love,
and just how deep?"

— June 27, 2012

Time Signature

For nearly a day
I have laid across
this slab of desert stone;

lonely, but not alone,
fixed upon the shadow
of your Love;

unhinged, it travels
from something steady
towards something unknown;

clutching your image
imagined, sticking its coastal
toe, perhaps, into a jetty;

I growl at my helpless heart;
missing the real you
too soon already.

      — October 4, 2012

Crossing the Line

Before you let me cross the line,
the distance great between us,
our best features muted, serrated
not drawn fine; purpose lay halved,
disabled by a chasm wide,
the two parts scraping on their sides.

Then you came into view
as close as this;
a part of me blew a kiss,
warming your senses,
but still it missed; until you
stooped to cradle a flower,
my nose appeared there, too,
at Fate's chosen hour.

Now we
linger, languid,
full of essence,
feeding off each other's presence,
Love stands near, binding us
with strands of time. . . and fear. . . and trust;
how strange this mindful calm that
shrinks the world into our palms,
a simple kiss, a powerful sign,
back and forth across the line.

— October 18, 2012

The Vanishing Point

Nothing to lose, lost Love.
Need I pump my maximus,
my pecs,
my upper arms,
my abs?
Tell me what you
need and I will
do it, counting ninety one...
ninety two... ninety three.
Nothing to lose, lost Love.
Tell me how to
take you, make you,
waste you, taste you,
do you all around.
Ah... there...
everything BUT love lost,
and can't be undone.
You are all but chasing after it,
you are prompted to run,
run after as it fades,
now slayed,
no love to lose,
it is all gone away.

— November 18, 2012

Breezy, Cheezy

To see
what the sea
washes upon you;
to air
what the air
tells me to do.
Oh, the waiting, the weighting.

— November 22, 2012

How Much?

How much
good looks
clever manliness,
shrewd dealings,
respectable wealth,
danger diligence,
prudent I.Q.,
uncontested cool
must I exude to swoon you,
yearbook girl grown up
and jaded by sixty yules.

Yes, unblessed I come to you
perhaps too late in life.
Undressed, all confessed,
my social virtues
unwashed.
Still. . .
I quest.
I endeavor to reach your heart
in hopes of learning
just how much.

— November 22, 2012

Overlooked

Did you eschew
Love anew,
for those too few
who bobbled the unknown,
the untouchable,
that promise that was You?

— December 7, 2012

Modern Morse

I.L.U.
I.I.L.W.Y.
When they ask why, I.
nominate U. for the
big B. of L. I. will WILL,
orate, parade, &
pantomime yor best
in the sacred bk.
of 'What a Nut.'
If I.m. yor Achilles
of L.O.L.,
U. r. my muse
as much as I can use
at any 1 time.
I would like to
dance & Friend
yor mind, yor lips,
yor cosmo sips. Is it
greedy 2 want 2 W?
My Invite: plse come do
the I.L.U.

— December 2012

A Walk in the Words

Love, love, love.
I wanted love.
I demanded that she say it.
And I was willing
to take a long walk
into the woods to get it.

Love. One of the great pertinences.
Love has heft. Anything
less would invalidate.
"Why do you need it?"
"Well, I... I just
don't see any wiggle room."

To answer would
be like trying to explain China.
To be less than loved.
I did not wish to be an asterisk,
a pretend person in the yes, no, whatever,
orbiting a more accommodating status.

I demanded an upgrade.
I wanted to face her – to be
rejiggered above the who, what,
when, where, and why.
I wanted love. I had pursued Love's label
from Point Hope to Prudhoe Bay.

I supposed I had swung too far.
And then she faced me, and she said,
"I love you, Johnny loveless,
but first I gotta like you."
And I knew she was
in the real.

She was more than a glitter girl.
She was part of the penultimate.
She was a grandiloquent, yearning me
into her arms and into her legs, and
into the way is the way.
She was huggable.
She became my friend and nothing else mattered.
"I like you," she said, "and if you wish,
bring Love along."

— December 20, 2012

Upon Making It Thru December

All riddles solved,
all puzzles puzzled,
restless doubts and snow-weighted calm
in their bed; mistletoe falls
upon our heads, and kiss engraved sonnets
still say what they always said.

A new beginning for us;
we are in the "new;"
and I am totally
in love with you!

— December 31, 2012

Friends and Lovers

Jaci and Bill always game,
exchanged letters
in each of their names;
Jaci became 'Jill,'
and Bill became 'Baci,'
so different,
yet still the same.

— January 23, 2013

Love Chores

SHARING yourself
with me – your son, your mother,
your friends, your brothers,
your house, your money,
everything sad and
everything funny;

UNTYING your
value purse, your childhood verse,
your carnal words,
strange, uncouth – your
undiluted sense of truth;

EXPOSING your
guarded sides,
your jeweled facets of risk
now collide. I bundle them
your bales of flaw,
heavy and present now,
and completely raw;

EXHIBITING yourself
in exhibitesque,
playful, ungarnished true burlesque,
the flowers faint in disarray
at your every jest
at what they saw,
exuding scented
"ah, ahh, ahhh's."

READING to me,
with enchanted voice,
the way to sleep an easy choice,
nestling amongst the author's leaves,
nocturnes from the air you breathe,
sated by this day that's through,
loving all these things you do.

— November 24, 2012

Trivial Convivial

Real Love Time is
relative, and understood
only by True Lovers.
Five years, ten years,
half a life time – mere
deviations the vessel True
Love carries before its
radioactive half life begins?

Infirmed, wrinkled, gray,
our once ordinary love
no longer trivial,
now an ancient tapestry
so well sewn with the
enduring strength of
Love's soft ropes of silk.
Still, in the Time of Real
Love, it is but a rug.

— February 1, 2013

Philosophe

Love and what to do about it.
The thought never occurs
until it happens.
Some small part of the Soul
the size of a suitcase bomb
finally blows, ending all else.
Yes, painful, if it is real,
Love's submission,
ruling in grotesque ways,
challenging our questionable
place in every detail, and what
revelation's light does with it.

— February 9, 2013

Unarguable

Dear Boy you did drift,
wandering hard against the wind,
some blood on your saddle,
not fit for allegiance,
unwilling to embrace
the myths and allegories
called upon you,
your suffering, poems,
your tattered beliefs –
your get-up-and-leave.
Oh Fine Young Man
no one could hate you,
your polite ways
of giving lip service,
you're going through the motions,
kissing every blarney stone.
Wake Up! Rider of the Silver Grey,
sleeping with your horse
under a scratching bridle
and matching sky,
your eyes still blue
but your urges obediently dying,
your stories quietly corralled
into life two thirds gone.

Then... she arrived
on her own lonely horse,
towing you out of your stumble.
She looked past your sudden love dumbness.
You chased her without a single rational
thought,
shouting "kaplooey!" at your solitude.
You wish you had met her sooner.
That's what grinning's all about.

— February 14, 2013

The Pledge

If you learned
that a plain old man
made the sun rise;
and that a plain old woman
made it set; as a
love for each other
not consummated yet;

Would you still
defiantly cling
to ordered things,
if Love perfect
needed your help to
arrive on time?

When then one
uncalculated day,
looking up you see your
deed painted wide in its
crucial palette sky…
will you not drop your
schedule, dear,
and pay the Love still
in the arrears.

Preamble to Jaci

True Love
and I walked
out from the density
of noise
and expectations,
stopping to lay,
our escape poised
beneath a friendly oak.
"What are you
dreaming?" she
asked finally,
our eyes stroked and
hammocked by the
folds of fallen leaves.
"Love, love.
Tree, tree."

The Last Martini

When I left you
I didn't know I was leaving,
I didn't mean to be deceiving
though truth had not been my guide,
something got me to take that ride
to this new place that feels so true.

Trust me sweet love,
when I climbed aboard that train
I felt no loathing, no hatred, no pain.
Forty years we've played our game;
the rituals, the rendezvouses, not a moment of shame;
no bruising, no battling, no ledges, no shoves.

You wouldn't like it where I am, it's been said,
out here on the lamb,
using reel feelings to get out of a jamb.
This place is about the pain of getting real;
when life gets edgy as part of the deal,
no darling no, you can't reach for the meds.

The conductor walks past, he gets the gist,
he asks me if I'm ready for my journey to start.
"I know," he says, "that you broke her heart."
Then he blurts it out, the prophet's rhyme
as the train wheels click in perfect chimes,
"gin, straight up, an olive and a twist."

Mile after mile in the left you behind,
good times we shared, still elixing in the glass,
the company we kept, the feelings we amassed.
You knew enough to turn me away.
Only in my dreams will you ever say,
"Till the next time darling, I'll be O.K."

And What Then?

Neither of you
would bring it up,
even as waiting merely
whittled the thing
into an emotional sabre,
inching us backwards to
an unavoidable leap.

He went first,
blurting out in bed,
"your demands," as you
put it, softly, remorsefully later,
laboring in a barely audible voice
that "you didn't think
that you could. . ."

The hesitation in itself
declared a load too heavy,
". . . the over burden
that unmistakably
called Love quits. . ." leaving him to
speculations, lowering himself
all the way down.

"How many kisses will be missed
because they were disavowed?"
he'd ask, not yet in his cups.
"How will the birds be fed,
bedtime verses still be read,
how much adoration
to your womanhood will go unsaid?"

He, too, paused, he could
think of one: "And how will you
dream of our growing essence left undone?"
All left unanswered.
Love is not a negotiation,
so she broke his heart
through hesitation.

To The Bone

Before the sun get down
in Martini Town,
before good looks get a looking
and the best horses get a booking,
and before our love making gets cooking...
we've only started to fool around.

Once again that moment comes,
my bliss takes a dive
into a pool of glum,
after the talk, talk,
and the touch, touch,
clinging to that image of you
I love so much.

Time to pay my "too long
since I've seen you" dues,
you're never behind
any of the doors I choose,
don't wanna win you,
just don't wanna lose,
it's a bad case of the
convoluted game show blues.

Limerick

A pig and spider
were lovers,
they lived decades
under the covers.
On their graves
carved the voice
of their life long
sweet choice,
we choose Love
if you grant us our druthers.

Your Face
(for Sue)

YOUR FACE.
YOUR FACE seeks the history of us.
Your unleveled eyes;
your rushmore nose;
your daliesque lips and raven cheeks,
each a player within
our story; separately viewed
through animus, how then we cast
ourselves circling the other with
sniffing, yielding to hungry, sometimes
ravenous lust – and then, now, dare we love?
Your face reveals the parable of us. It lively leads
your wild promenade – your rivulets, your
symbiotic cliff of monuments,
patiently carved and creviced.
I have learned how to approach, mask removed,
swaying before your face, each act of intimacy,
each increment of trust.
Your face; an archeology.

— July 22, 2014

Of What Do you Dream

Of what do you dream
when the world turns in its card;
when the rivers have rivered
and the mountains have steeped,
when you've sculpted who you are
and have become what you keep;
when the last bird of flight
returns to its nest,
leaving the burdens of light
for what's under its chest;
and all lays quiet the mind at rest;
of what do you dream?

— July 24, 2014

With You in the Land of Georgia O'Keefe

. . . that dreamy look you share,
the voluptuae, the nippolous
budding overlooks,
your languid valley,
your bold rain forest, your svelteness
within the borders of your Rubenesque.

I roam about the two of you – we merge
in the me, the her,
the us, the you. . . you paint
the words not found in any
book, and like her, so dreamy
with that dreaming look.

Now, later, you the nude artists
read out loud some numb critic
gloating, braining,
sawing away at
your lingering largesse, saved
only by your 'aliving' of the dreaminess.

— July 31, 2014

Because We Saw Us Naked

We played to each other as thespians might,
drawn by stage design and dialogue – as
some other man clutched you for balance.
Your adlibbed clichés and newspaper fluff
went on with the soft playful patter
of intermittent rains.

Then we got naked.
The language changed, the naked
comfort and new meaning
staying and playing,
swaying all feeling and purpose.

Sometimes as we lie there,
the only props in Life's
big new nature,
reciting scenes from the
ongoing us – you insist again
upon my first perception.

"But do it in a single word," you say,
now that earlier summaries of your
postures and sparkles wear thin.
"scintillating!" Accepted, it stays,
now that I live with you naked.

— August 5, 2014

Upon Flattering the Flowers

The Tulip bulbs arrived
precisely cut, in shallow boxes
carefully constructed and air holed,
a fitting carriage for the genetic
wonders cradled inside.

On a Fall day predicting Spring,
the pods got escorted from
their registered cart and planted
in a bed of exquisite mulch, feathered
and churned for these royal botanicals.

Hundreds of years of documented lineage
did not disappoint, jutting rapid growth,
their arrowed green arms, lanky lucent
olive bud stems – hiding for now
a well-orchestrated fanfare.

Bursting forth from their drapes,
exactly engineered super models
appeared on time, in vivid designer
hooped skirts of unblemished
reds and yellows and deep hued whites.

These beau willowy ideals pranced
in the runway breeze, soliciting awe,
their tall necked 'look' pushing back
all bramble, all lessor human touch that
threatened to blemish their portrayal.

Then you appeared, abruptly crashing,
stumbling gorgeously into frame,
unfazed by your own creation
of sinewy parts, strung together
with lips and lass.

I watched from the gardener's shadow
your innocence limbering to its knee,
your forged nose landing on the nearest petal.
I saw the disturbed parade turning, craning,
leaning in towards you.

— August 26, 2014

Sue, You, Sue

On the steppes of an invisible pyramid
our lips met, cautiously. . .
then NOT.
Your kisses have continued.
Suddenly. . . I AM NOT.
No longer
the endless rugged Plains,
nor the anthem,
nor the marching band,
nor the baton discharging war
and the thump of its music.
Suddenly I AM
only and all the gift of your love.
WE LIFT its secret up the narrow treads,
the risers.
Opportunities to descend
disappear – so little room to stand
on its point, where air is sipped.
From the Base of this massive
light headed design,
I, humbled by your love,
i am not.

— August 10, 2014

Sue in September

How I have waited
for this moment
above the points
of the hand hewn saw,
watching the warm paint dress
the raw dove tall joints.
All day I have worked to reach
this stopping place, away from hammerings
and fitted forms. I have craved
the inexactness of our fingers locking,
leaning against a wall with you,
savoring the small progresses of
our hopeful estate.
Now... under a quiet canopy roof,
beneath a throw of stars
we muzzle with the rustle of sheets
in the late night look-see,
where nothing is cut, and nothing is dried,
a mouth of words bubbling from the slurry
of our wet kissy in the wee,
"I love You, as You love Me."

— September 15, 2014

Nuance

YOU KISSED ME
differently.
The opening sun
across the run of
coo cooing morning doves
was to be expected.
But not this.
I am excited, untold;
should I be wary,
or should I be bold?
Still, it was a kiss,
and I'm feeling anything but old.

— November 1, 2014

The Highness

. . . of it all. Yes, more human
acts of mutual exploitation are possible;
like this – your female folds
and my muscle,
shall never be remiss
as long as we ball into our tangle.

You get it, I know – the adding,
the multiplying – the exponential
quality of kisses – OUR kisses – our
wet wishes of lust and love's dishes.
Simplicity, enormity, even guano and scat,
Continuous, messy, piled high – what's wrong with that?

— December 12, 2014

Letter to a Former Love

"I've 'fallen in' with someone special. I, the selfish one, care about her. I believe she feels the same towards me. I get a better sense of what I am searching for – what it means to be human when I am with her. She's an artist. She acknowledges the 'You' and the 'It' in every person and everything.. She tends to the daily rhythms that keep her healthy. She adheres to the small requirements necessary to maintain order and comfort and shelter.

This Wonder Woman inspires all around her with her humor, her wit, her empathy, her engaging curiosity. I have never seen her neglect the eye contact required for the maintenance and enrichment of human dignity.

All of this she brings together with such a combustion – I am propelled toward the beauty of Her. And she is absolutely beautiful to me. I know that every nuance experienced because of her is a blessing.

In short and if that were possible,
I would choose to be her.

— January 9, 2015

One Thing

Love changes all,
and I, previously slogging
from one life wound to another,
would never have healed.

I would never have seen
the glisten and the sheen
beyond my paper cuts.

Your love changes me abruptly,
lasting, deeply, starting me over
to feel flushed and
butterfly chasing foolish.

Love changes I,
previously forgetting to wiggle my toes.
I now know, love changes all.

— January 27, 2015

See. Generation Gap Haiku. See?
(for Sue)

That flower
opened like a cheap date
looking for a bee, she
cared less that we air brushed
ourselves from intrusion,
not worrying whether
true digital rumors spread faster than
false ones; that twitters peak just
before earthquakes – this life of them
we opt from, as you and me
skitter, waltzing wonderfully without itching,
exposing our wrinkly-assed
selves at the dance of the mindful
and the free.

— March 23, 2015

Vampire Valentine

Still, still
you do more than endless full moons
to rile the blood waves.
My heart slaves for you,
surrendering motive.
Your voice does that jump start thing
as you amazon over me,
pumping and pounding me,
taunting me, bidding me
to rise up inside of you;
that you aren't kidding.
This time you will it, and
you know it to be true.
I'm already and blissfully dead for you.
Still, still.

First Draft of Love

You are the story of us.
You have laid by me,
played by me,
stayed granite side-by-side.
You giggled and guffawed,
when I only knew to laugh.
You shouldered my cries,
You have wagged your fingers
in my eyes.
You won, you placed, you showed
with social grace – you proved there
is no valid reason to lie – your epic
one liner remains, "My oh my!"
You are the story, the first line
and last.
You are the story.
You are the glory.

— Just Before March, 2017

4
Dissonance and Discontent

IN 1971, FOUR cousins in the Mann Family shared a correspondence, with the youthful purpose of finding meaning in our lives and the prospect of living some more. Cousin Rick chose to emulate his father's ardent capitalism, but as a soulful landlord providing reasonably priced live-work rentals to artists and artisans. Cousin David became an articulate card carrying member and active recruiter for the Progressive Labor movement within the Community Party. Cousin Dottie turned to evangelical religion, working her way up the hierarchy of The Way Ministry.

My path veered towards travel and adventurism, poetry, personal letters, and hedonism. Following some intense political and religious confrontations between the four of us during those searching times, I put the following lyrics to song, then stuffed them in my wallet, retrieved only recently:

> The pill, the bomb,
> the Viet Cong,
> something's always
> going wrong;
>
> Bureaucracy democracy,
> someone's making fun of me,
> a ballot box to
> vote for Jesus Christ;
>
> All I've got is
> love, love, love,
> and love, love, love
> won't be enough.

Now, approaching fifty years later, I believe we cousins are less inclined to activism, and more prone to agree that living in America is becoming a nasty business, due to the fact that our government treats its own people as badly as it treats people all around the world.

Before we can effectively corner the beast and change ourselves for the better, it seems likely that we need to express our dissatisfactions visibly, tolerantly, openly, publicly, vehemently, and honestly.

For me, for now, that means, "Poems of Dissonance and Discontent."

Out

It is late in the day
and I am unwarmable,
my feet having become
wooden blocks against obligation.
A light dust is gathering
upon me in the motionless.
My defiant mind
detaches, fixed into
its uneventful look-out.
The birds dig deeper
for seeds muddied down,
undaunted by any unnatural
fizz of clichés.
It is late in the day of my unfeeling,
as the "I" runs out of
mood to face the opposition.

Tragic Noblesse

We are under the bridge
sleeping, as
you've done these last four years.
So kind of you
to let me later boast, "Yeah. . .
I've lived among the homeless."
I will wear
the Badge of Cool
at black tie affairs
for the likes of you. . .
you who will never
see any of it,
and never care.
You are so natural, comfortable
in your unnatural state. Our
one night 'life' under the bridge
smells real, over your
coffee can fire.

you asked me to sleep-over,
to brave the clever trappings
of your austerity, listening to
who you once were... before
you were not even
a number anymore.
And only then, because
I imposed,
you shared through angry eyes
your True Love's demise,
her leaping from the expressway
over this very spot you have sworn
never to leave...
and then the police came.

Those Who Count

They started by
knocking down slammers,
third of July at
second and Wall,
sun setting upon the
bloated mammon bull,
its hooves anchored
into the money currents,
its sovereign shadow
swaggering amidst the
swarm of suits at O'Shaunesey's,
glistening with smarm,
each other blathering of
mega-million commissions, the
artfulness of their deals,
sleeves and slang rolled up
in puffy banter as to
the merits of extracting fortunes,
whether by fish netting
the multitude
or by single algorithmic
triumphs over miscalculating whales,
and how one of their own
just now notched
his first billion "with a B!"
A brashling tore at his share of raw meat
heaped at the trough of braggadocio,
"They BEG us to burn

holes in their pockets!"
He too, stoked his animus,
washing down a pig testicle
to the raunchy roars and sodden Latin clichés.
And there in the din
and the smoke,
and all the fat talk
of buying and selling
entire nations – a thorny hand went
up in their mosh pit, and
stayed up, creating an edgy lull.
"I don't suppose
a single one of you titans
have ever poured
a farthing of your own money."
As they suddenly loomed large
about her – she must have
believed they would only have
smirked and carried on
at her bunned, marmish hair,
her retired broach, the stink
of her fume – her oldness.
They might only have restrained
themselves rudely, mocking her
high-brow and leave it at that.
But being in no mood
to come down that far from
their exuberance, they merrily

carried her and her shrill admonitions
instead, to a foot bridge
over a back alley wash,
pinching a penny to her tongue
before giving her the heave ho,
competing then to caricature
her fatal descent, as if it were
the weekend play-by-play,
concluding with the beer nuts.
It would have made the headlines
if it had occurred during her era.
But it did not.
"What have we become?"
The Fourth of July font
came fairly large,
but overshadowed by the
unrestrained cravings
of yet another gilded age,
this one feeling inconvenienced
by the usual marching bands
and a float parade,
down the Avenue of the Americas.

— May 10, 2013

Big Game

I needed a furlough.
I lay in the tall grass
of the Kalahari,
away from the marauding madness,
my country on one of its
blood for oil campaigns.
Would not a camera
commune with nature
clear my name?
When through my safari lens
invading males used a
strategic breeze to plunder
the neighboring lion pride, making certain
all the young died, while I watched
on my own full stomach.
"Alexander! Alexander!" shouted
the guide, pointing his spear
toward the most mighty.
My heart beat wildly
but I did not cry, as it had
previously been pointed out
to me, that *this* killing was not senseless
and therefore not the same.

— April 3, 2013

Golden Gate

A kit came early in life,
the instructions and pieces
simple, lean, filled with cliché.
Obey the law.
Be diligent and clean.
Work to the bone.
Buy. Buy. Buy something feel good
every single day.
The Game of Life
luring, singing to the gullible me,
promising wondrous hypnotic things,
of making dollars out of dimes,
of putting muscle into maxims,
one shovel at a time.

The staircase of splendored
booty – mine for
the competing; the coveting;
the recruiting of others
willing to become 'lifers,'
lifers like me. It has taken
quite a life to see and be seen,
strapped as we are to the
Zero Tolerance Machine,
down it looks at minors and menials,
the less motivated
coming out of the thing
as resigned, inconvenient waste,

still present, unpleasant to consider, but
mostly invisible to fresh, dazzled,
upward yearning eyes.
My division of Life Persuasion Inc.
collapsed under its own weight,
its rule makers' greed too great,
castles crammed with treasure hoard
delivered by monopoly boards,
and too few left to play.
I, old, witless and wasted,
fallen out from the scheme
before I could reach my implanted dream,
shuffle with other tail draggers
towards the bridge, still clutching
our empty bags.

The numbers are up this year
I am told, as we ledge decidedly
into the Bay's leeward wind.
From our inglorious precipice,
I see more gullibles below,
diligently laying stone to
yet another pyramid, having no
idea what they cannot see
in a world they cannot own.
How desperately they need
to be saved by a super tree.
For the record, my number is
one thousand five hundred
and eighty three.

— Summer 2013

Walking in the Garden, Naked

Carbon Credits, dead rivers,
still borns, lymphomas,
his coal powered lights,
transformers across the grid,
he cut open the ultraviolet skies,
with his mind and
by his hand.

Finally frightened
by nothing left to destroy,
he closed his eyes
at the joy of walking
in the only garden left, naked.
Naked with you.

The Adultery of ID

Carbon Credits.
Dead Rivers.
Stillborns.
Lymphoma.
Coal powered lights and machines,
all across the grid.

Insatiable Planet ID
does not breathe – it spews
the bile of Consumption,
using oceans as its toilet.
ID pierces the sky dome
with unyielding dioxide swords.

Finally the Ice Cap is conquered
by ID's hand, and
by ID's mind,
watching triumphant,
Nature vanquished,
the top of the world topples.

Frightened ID.
No joy in nothing left to destroy,
when ID is through
savaging Saint Earth walking
in the only garden left, walking
naked in the garden with you.

The Last Hurrah

You've stabbed good men
with cold quill pens, shouting
"They have a right to know."
And did the Public know your motives
my journalistic friends?

... stabbed good men
with jagged pride, with hate,
with wormy goals in mind, well
what the hell let's call it sick ambition.

And when what little
civilization remains
is completely gorged upon itself,
by your baitings, beratings, your
cheap-shot investigating..
... you may have the last hurrah.

Hurrah the new journalism.
The verbal thugs. That gang
without an afterthought. Shall we
say they tore up a town, searching
for their own integrity?

Look up might warriors of the pen:
even your vultures are puking...

— 1986

Counting the Dead

When my job came easier
it was known as The Body Count.
A dead life considered appropriately messy
in normal times of war, revered
and sent home – is now delayed by conventions.
My bonuses come from
crisp photos of dead children
under fifteen, and men and women
over sixty – sorted, culled from obliterated
combatants of twenty to twenty nine,
each corpse expected to pull its weight
among those attempting to place
a more humane face on war.
This is what I do, tailgating gurneys in
the wards and the morgues.
I anger many as I inventory
who matters as a legitimate target,
and who does not,
correcting status reports for
registered hierarchies of the dead,
for the war machines and their patrons,
down to teeth and bones and body parts.
Do not throw stones at me.
It is complicated. I correlate and validate.
I am the ledger man handing questionnaires
at funerals. I do not start these wars.

— August 9, 2014

On the Outs

After years of doing
the 'out and about,'
I woke, disturbed by their
airs and powers.
They were pushing me out,
with a deliberate shove,
I the oblivious, the old man,
'the grey one,' irrelevant,
something to be filed under
'in lieu of.'
Yes, still hinged to the War
and the Dissent; but this
was more than pining for
long fins and massive grills
with chromed teeth.
People had stopped listening.
They were younger and so many
of them, so fewer of me,
letting me know with indifference,
that this was now their time,
their entitlement.

Was I sleep walking to assume
they would include me,
would serve civility
without ice?
I once had a nick name,
I was dynamic with a wide range.
I used to be cool.
Have I truly become
the sad realization of suffering fools?
Am I the only one now dissenting
this one small change?

— Summer 2013

Failure to Disclose

On the occasion
of a waterfront picnic
my love and I found ourselves
swallowed by a flag waving swarm,
there to welcome
the comings home,
some whole
some not so,
(the dead arrived separately,
also with flags
but without fanfare).

Coincidentally
my love and I previously
saw some of the men
signing for duty
outside a box store,
gleefully departing with
gift-wrapped recruiter promises
of pay, new skills,
glory of course,
and glamour travel.

Now they come
down the gangway,
with those eyes made lifeless
by seeing too much.
My love and I

did not hold flags, and were
frowned upon for wondering out loud
whether or not the broken and half hearted
(many of whom no longer
held the stomachs for patriotic sing-alongs),
had been told that
"For God and Country" also meant
killing, and carnage, and rape, and torture,
and massacre of children and mothers, and
old people who did nothing more
than give their entire lives,
in the hope of one day watching
a grandchild play at their feet.

Now the warrior mercenaries
in their bleached coming home skivvies
and their lifeless eyes,
mustered mightily to buck up
and not betray protocol
by spilling guts
at so joyous, this occasion.

Even in our grass stained feet
and holding a picnic blanket,
my love an I could see that
the flag wavers had not been told
more horror would
accompany the comings home.
Someone should have warned
(at least in small print)
that cars would be driven into sidewalk crowds;
that families would be exposed

to madness, sleeplessness, night sweats and
night screams, and suicides, and
murder suicides, and syndromes that
make a once perfectly healthy man
yelp into the fetal position, at the mere 'chirp'
of a smoke detector;
and that scummed up hero hospitals would
engulf their cots with roaches and mold,
back here at the home of the brave.

Would the fine print
have warned that our invading armies
no longer deliver
nor return home with patriotism
(assuming they ever did);
that your god and flag and country are
no better for, no more secure, no more
looked up to or loved by enemies,
for all this killing that you did?

War no longer rhymes.
War is for the low humming
monotones of drones, and for
mercenaries who return
with lifeless eyes.
When you come back, will they tell you
something more awaits?
Will they warn you that
we should all be wary
when war comes marching home?

A King, A Kaiser, A Czar

O please, O please Mr. President, don't speak for me.
I have laid down my weapon, my vote, that I not be
included in the Great War, the Good War, the
War That Saves The World, the
War That Makes The World Safe
for the ones who vote.
O please O please Mr. President,
as you notch the bodies with heroic harrahs,
count me among the cowardly, the difficult,
the opinionated, the suffering.
Please don't speak for me
as you reason that war is human,
as you reach back to find a history
where war is guiltless, unavoidable,
necessary and the fault of others.
See? I have laid down my vote before you.
I lie under your horse.
O please O please Mr. President,
grandly give my vote to your war lords,
your arms makers, your crown princes
of banking, your corporate prompters,
your food poisoners.
O please O please Mr. President,
deny me clean air, but don't speak for me.
My hands raised high, I have buckled,
I have wearily laid down my vote,
no longer on the side of victors.

— July 2014

Sanibel Sketch 1
(at Sandy Bird)

Sand grass,
Saw grass,
Wax myrtle trees;
Marshes,
Channels,
Wetlands, lees;
Mosquito fish
and leather leaves,
black birds dressed
in dappled wings,
from reeded brush
the cardinal sings;
Island's message
before the gale,
most things have
their price, but
not everything's for sale.

— 2012

Sanibel Sketch I
(at Sandy Bend)

Sandgrass,
saw grass,
wax myrtle trees;
Marshes,
Channels,
wet lands, lees;
Mosquito fish
and leather leaves;
black birds dressed
in dappled wings,
from reeded brush
the cardinal sings;
Island's message
before the swale,
most things have
their price,
not everything's for sale.

w. Frederick
3/30/12

Legend

The universe was disappearing,
an unintended consequence
of the digital,
our egos slowly
dissolved by speeds
too fast for face book.
We began to stutter in tech-speak,
no longer able to think on our feet,
or claim original thought,
each nuance
instantly covered by glittering flecks
of data, heaped too high for recycle.
When one final viral brain freeze
zombied the self-inflicted masses,
a grim-faced raft of luddites
regressed to the sea,
grasping for the old wooden analog world
singing,
loving,
holding on,
bobbing in the swell,
praising god at the sight of land,
only to find themselves
at the bottom of a well.

— April 4, 2013

Lifeboat

Your steel brittle hull
breaking apart
like just another temporal thing,
shatters our icy senses,
ringing death's bell
with each cry in the silencing sea.
Lucky, alive, it does not feel that way,
even in our lifeboat.
Lifeboat?
Your disappearing remnants, Terrible T,
we the well-pleased ambassadors of
your masterful machine
float now, little more than bilge,
your ambergris, something to be
distilled into something else.
We do not feel valuable,
prying away the weighty grips
of hangers on, as we numbly
pray for a 'safer' haul.
Survive?
What severance do we take back
to undo your broken trust?
Oh, answer there! Our lifeboat refitted
to a stronger, better, bigger ship,
our hats and clothes souvenired as 'keeple.'
Oh salient truth: parts over people.

— April 2012, 100th Anniversary, Sinking of the Titanic

ELEPHANT
(about the size of things)

Is it strange?
We did not see either of them.
Both occupied the room as we
moved, and talked, and touched
throughout our lives... staring
through the diminutive,
unaware of the gargantuans
but inches away.
Is it magic?
This ability of titans to ignore
the agitated and the poor,
remarkably blind to
anything larger than they.
Shall we pledge?
"To reducing the elephant
and growing the ant."
That we might meet
somewhere in the middle.

— Revised July 28, 2014

New Math

In the good times before the era of analysts and military
protagonists – they simply called it 'the body count.'
Eventually combatants, civilians, and collateral damage.
Decades – I have been doing this – I AM
the body counter as they gurney past me
in the hospital wards and morgues.
There is more at stake now besides
missiles and mortar rounds, and
'pay onto Ceasar,' and 'pay onto God.'
It is the tithing and the tax man counting
the children, the army, a martyr under
forty five, the women, an old man now
eighty five, determined by what they were
doing at the time, and for what purpose, and for whom,
as they were obliterated, part of the new War Math.
This is what I do, how I sort. I... exchequer,
the logger, the ledger man in the basement
with no windows to distract me, an emissary,
a number cruncher for every invader as the assaults occur,
the assassinations, the bombs sprinkled here and there.
Ho hum your inconveniences as you
grocery shop, as you take comfort in
the Genevas, the Rights Watchers, the World
Court, the International Humanities – as you
wait impatiently for my numbers.
It's complicated. I just count the corpses.
I do not start the wars.

— August 6, 2014

Not Like You

We are sick, scared, and dying,
from this evil that seems to follow you
after you fall from the sky
in colorless clothes that
hide your faces.
We do not need you
to tell us we are sick. We see
you tremble as we bleed from our eyes.
Why do you bring this dark, wretched,
merciless THING to us?
We have only knives and stones
and machetes and logs over the roads,
to push back your cold metal objects
and your songless voices from some distant star.
Your killer men point weapons at
people we love. We are not like you.
You are afraid of mothers and fathers
who hold the dying, crying, terrified children.
What is wrong with you?
We have nothing you could want.
Go away. Leave us to
weep, surrounded by kindness.
We are not like you.

— August 6, 2014

Not a Brave Man

I am not a brave man.
When the platitudes of
work and worthiness, and
perseverance and the requirements
of Americanism corner me
in school rooms, chapel pews, diner
booths and t.v. lounges – I run.

I run from water fountain predators,
their sure things, their epistles, their
guarantors and guarantees,
their sell you anything behind
every single door.
I am not a brave man
in the vacuum of medicine wagons
and ho downs, and sage brush
advice. . . anything that riles fear
and promises to be 'good' for me.

I run. I run from the minions of valor.
I the brave man not,
I do not ride the passionate divide.
I am not a mover, shaker, nor opinion maker.
I the coward am.
I fear flags, flag makers, and flag wavers.
I cannot, I am not,
I am not a brave man.

—— July 31, 2014

~~DIGGERS~~ EXCAVATORS
~~SIXTEEN GRAVES~~

So now you have come
to kill us ~~finally~~,
because you believe death is final.
How disgusted you ~~must feel~~ are,
standing over the last of us,
~~these final moments of~~ history, unjust
tiptoeing about our corpses,
littered where we fell,
eyes bulging open in smelly
consumes ~~estuaries~~ of shallow body fluid.
For centuries you ~~have been~~ took
taking us in ~~your water ships~~, with your shackle hooks
your air ships, craft,
ripping and sucking
life and love from the moorings where we were born
from ~~our once buried fathers~~ from the
~~our once burial place~~,
put ~~now laid barren as you put~~ fires
to our hiding places, tending
your intellect ~~our forests, as you turn us~~ as you time after
your fingers ~~into waste.~~ time tossed us into waste
stand in you How you must deplore
witnessed into ~~disposal process~~ the body disposal process,
that killing us is ~~so~~ messy
~~in these last hours,~~ the ~~horror~~ horrid ghoulish mess
trenching us down and deep,
fearing even our dogs
will dig us and ~~rub us in your face~~ stir your cleansing legs.
How careful you are not to touch, takes
because you are the ~~rippers~~,
the ~~takers~~, the ~~suckers~~ ritual undertakers (pain stakers)
from a ~~place~~ room that never touches.
Five, ten, one thousand ~~deaths~~ kills (graves) paper trail
each hour from the plagues ~~the~~ boothill martingale
of your doing. We see you gristmill nightingale
urging us to die ~~faster~~ clean
during this time of your inconvenience, coffin nail
We do not suffer your ~~not snails~~ veil death
churchy lullabies and fairy tales. the has no
We know you believe death is final grail nail
Just as you took down so many peoples
~~who didn't fit into~~ your prayers, cortail
we too are stacked ~~in four piles~~ layered detail
~~an human~~ debris, an entire culture entail
hosed down with chlorine, exhale
then removed from view prevail
~~a once beautiful people~~ once beautiful flowers no resale
now forced to live inside of you. retail
wage scale
eight penny nail wags its tail
still betrayal
economy of scale

Excavators

So now you have come
to kill us finally,
because you believe death is final.
How disgusted you are,
standing over the last of us,
the ashes of our history unjust,
tiptoeing about our corpses,
littered where we fell,
eyes bulged open in smelly
consumes of shallow body fluid.
For centuries you took us
with your shackle hooks,
ripping and sucking
life and serenity shorn
from the moorings where we were born,
now laid bare by the fires
put to our hiding places,
your indelible terror
witnessed in our faces.
How you must deplore
the disposal process,
the horrid ghoulish mess,
you trench us down and deep,
fearing even our dogs
will dig us and spoil your cleansing logs.
How careful you are not to touch,
because you are the takers,
the rippers, the cultural undertakers

from a realm that never touches.
Five, ten, a thousand kills
each hour, the plague gristmill
of your doing. We see you
urging us to die clean
during this time of your inconvenience.
We do not suffer your
churchy lullabies and fairy tales.
We know you believe death is the final grail.
Just as you took down so many peoples
not fitting of your prayers,
we too are stacked and layered,
an unsightly debris, an entire culture
hosed down with chlorine,
then removed from view,
a once beautiful people
now forced to live inside of you.

— October 15, 2014

Falsely Accused:
Looking Back, History Rearranged

Rhubarb over the hole in the bubble,
the woe-is-me's came to the trouble,
then henny pens went on a rant,
trying to ban deodorant.
Some hormonal teen deranged,
threatened us with climate change,
when out of the night and into the blue,
came a man like me and a lot like you,
changing a bulb in a cirrus c33
"there's suet in this thing," he cried out loud
"Not CO2... there's water vapor in this poo!"
It's water cooling not sunshine heating
that caused the kid to take a beating?
Coal plants, diesels, and aerosols
off the hook? Heads will roll!
"No, but the troposphere you can't be cheating,
shows jets, and crops, and yards and damns
are the real culprits in the global jam."
So THAT'S the thing we need to fear?
"It's many things, and pardon my zeal,"
Wisdom butted in with a humble face,
to the rescue and offering grace,
"before any answers go into the till,
IT'S TIME WE ALL GOT VERY REAL."

— Halloween 2014
(for Stoney)

The Quickening

August arrived on the tail end
of a desert monsoon's whiplash;
the ground had no sponge left in it
and the arroyos flooded, sucking in
a west side Phoenix kid on a bike;
the precariousness of nature.
If not for that – a stray bullet,
a rat born Hanta virus,
or an everyday predator
might have taken him.

In these times
everything occurs as a headline,
without taking a breath.

Village sized body counts
have become a dull thing.
We pretend they happen only
elsewhere, as we have come to expect
atrocity and depravity and greed,
filling up the spaces
of our indifference to sensation,
subdued by spectacle,
the entertainment value,
everything turning old quickly.

I don't want to agitate
this way, walking through life reacting to the
bombardment
of tragedy, desensitizing, running
through heavy traffic of
bad things happening, unable to
feel the good side of solitary moments
with the wind and the water and the sunlight
and the starlight, and the quiet sense of
the earth revolving.

Rat a tat tat!
Is the Earth coming apart,
or is it just me?

— October 6, 2014

Three Days Away from School

We marched.
We marched in tune
and out of step
with strangers we loved
in a Time that needed us.
No matter how far back
we stood from our Monument
Of Truth, it swayed nothing
from its relevance.
God maybe, Man for sure,
by the millions we marched,
jostling joyously,
joined at the hip
and at the lips.

We stunk.
Three days away from school,
stinking up crowded smoky rides,
easily guided toward True Moral
North, poised with
pure defiant purpose.
We found each other.
WE, a giant jubilant smoldering mass;
an entire generation taking it outside,
believing in something BIG,
an army of iconoclasts,
hacking down the sign posts
to murder, to waste, to inhumanity.

We marched together
on a shoe string
to the music,
to prose, feeling no fear
of missing out on our futures.

We marched together.
We would not be deterred.
WE the righteous war enders,
bringing to end the War that
was not the war of our fathers.
Our Fathers, from their silent
painful wary shadows
knew that WE,
the dissenting nation
were adrift,
but not on our way to hell.

I miss the march.
I would trade the whole
numbing pathos that followed
for the way THAT felt,
rather than another fifty years of hum drum,
our death by acquiescence.
Is it not with self-loathing
we trod this conveyor money belt?
Are we not sick of ourselves
buying shiny killer drones, pasting yellow

ribbons on military servers each day they
shore up our drooling consumption?
Is no hypocrisy too great?
Still we go to their walls
tracing our fingers along the fallen,
as that vile inhumane thing
within us, roars its nasty head again.

Oh dear brothers
and sisters,
we so neglected to
get at the roots.
Let us go outdoors
and find each other!
Let us march again.

                               — June 2013

You're Next

We winced as
the younger generation,
our children,
willingly gave over their digital
minds, entranced in their tablets,
all the while oblivious to
greedy global goblins
'thinning the herds' by
continental wars, starvation,
bad food and big disease.
We erred, thinking ourselves different.
After all, we marched, we rescued the flag
in the era of assassinations,
We earned our immunity, standing together,
hope warranted by a respect for the
documents protecting humanity.
But now, looking around and
seeing solidarity against mogulism gone,
we, the elders of rationalization, take ghastly
comfort in our abilities to forecast,
our sharpened sense of doom,
our 'stay' denied.
We know now that we have aged;
that we have failed to do
anything meaningful lately.
We hear the final words,
the amused voices of goon
as they casually come to collect us. . .

Over Done

As instructed,
over and over, many
times before, by one means or
another – we paddle along the thorny banks,
barely driveling soft ripples of the ebb and flow
by which we live.
In times of peace,
in times of war, generational
phrases come trotting out
tired and boorish, to carry us further.
We do what needs to be done,
nobly sacrificing mind after mind,
each one sentenced by the tyranny of words;
'auld lang syne' words; never say die words
driving us – wilted words desperately
charged with moral amps and
wattages – ordered to prop up
uncared for words no longer able to
stand on their own. Have we become
a drift of words struggling to convey meaning?
Are we these downtrodden words
sinking forward across formless sand – whole
civilizations scaffolded by words
now crumbling under scrutiny;
gutted zombie words with little
left to say, as we, mankind continue to
beat the idioms of clichés?

Word Club

"Nobody wants WAR,"
we the world
proclaim,
ordain,
through the lips of each
quorum, temple, mosque,
each steeple.

As unattended shame oozes
evenly over our cliché,
we take seriously the
words to defame – which
ones to keep,
to round or sharpen,
especially where the stakes run deep.

Our vigilant word smith crew,
anvils and justifies
why so many need to die;
what we say versus
what we do, tucked sincerely
within the tyranny of words,
"keep WAR, out people."

The War at Home

Egg flipper,
a whipper,
ice cream dipper,
the hardware store gripper;
bad little nipper
try to be chipper,
cause daddy's gone off to war.

Drinker,
sad thinker,
life on the brinker,
baby's a stinker,
car's a real clinker,
pawned my dear minker,
buck up and do your chores.

Sacrificer,
finger slicer,
child de-licer,
bedroom de-micer,
driveway de-icer,
patriot sufficer,
blood on the kitchen floor.

Grace Period expired,
bank man he liared,
patience retired,
fearful and wired,
laid off or fired,
no word, tired... tired,
not sure I can take any more.

Men at the door,
metal in the drawer,
bravery, honor, distinguished gore,
his life snuffed, mine ignored,
body bags, questions more upon more,
What For?
What For?

Seven Bromides
(thinly disguised)

1. LOOKING UP

If sky still looks like sky
we would not know why
our lives are giving at the seams,
unless Painter paints
a time not lost
in consciousness,
or someone's dreams.

2. BANG HEAD HERE

... is not the negative path
to happiness
nor the map to positivity.
Obey and clap, bang the bang,
shiv the shiv,
unless ye outlive
the daily counter intuitive.

3. GOAL ORIENTED

Governing power
foolishly lent,
dispatch the dissidents
with drones heavily sent.
Grind middle beings into poor,

with legal means hell bent,
cobbling great walls of our underachievement.

4. PUNISHING THE GUILTY

Money disappears, country in arrears,
no one accused, juries excused.
Who is guilty? What is just?
Castle builders seldom come in touch with us,
except to be heroic. Puppet News so stoic,
they 'search' to find the guilty. Now Mr.
Hand Made Threads, shoots a drifter in the head
for stealing some fruit. And THAT should do it.

5. SHORT SALE

He sits down with
his stuff on the lawn,
his equity gone,
Sheriff not done with him yet,
"America does not forget,"
as banker and shrewd buyers
haggle his debt.
Once driven, now head in his hands,
his plight a blight
across these lands, the shell game
only Wall Street understands,
and law dog with a boot to his chest,
"with your forgiveness
comes a bill from the I.R.S."

6. EVOLUTION

Cave Man
takes his club to me,
uses me, my sisters,
he gets what he wants.
He smothers us in sweat and stink.
He hunts us down when we run.
"Why tell me? I live
on the other side of the mound."
I am indentured,
I am a surf.
I slave away
my life, my woman, my babies.
I know you must squint
when you see us shackled to despair.
"Why do you dare
look me in the eye?"
I live over you now.
I own a plow.
I am modern, wage-driven
at a job I never did like,
making payments upon payments
that continue to spike.
I heard about less fortunate
diseased and unfed.
"Don't they know they need
more freedom over there?
"Why look at me?
Get back to work, jerk,
till you no longer need
to covet my jeans."

But what about suffering and injustice?
"I really don't care.
If you want to keep what you have,
don't make a scene.
I live in a brownstone.
You don't.
Know what I mean?"

7. ONE MORE INCH

If my body
can only cross
the arbitrary lines,
the perforated metes
and bloody bounds;
if more than my finger
can scale across this soggy map
to the other side of silent sensors,
snarling search dogs, and glum guns
telling me to go back;
if I can slither past badges and search lights,
and deep furrowed army boots, and gruff voices,
and thoroughly pensioned hands and hand cuffs
scraping the night terrain;
if one inch equals just fifty miles of all that and a
deadly indifferent desert – then I too will BE from
there, an invisible king lording the luxury to dream on
a full stomach of little things surely they have not yet bent
down to think about; if only I can just suffer the indignities
of one. . . more. . . inch.

Salvo

They rained on us. Not just the
white heat of war flares, but bejeweled
bursts and falling colored ropes of verse
entangling our simplistic means of artillery.
Vile verse militant, hot and revengeful;
despicable words of shining swords and
exploding things, attempting to make
our trenches ring with their sweet martyred dreams
of god and woman and life divine.
We, the humanitarians
felt naked in their light; unexpectedly
small, angry, bewildered.
All we had were guns, might, hypocrisy.
We came home defeated
by 'Al Qaeda Poems.'

5
Slam Poetry

SOME TIME AROUND 1992, I attended my first Slam Festival in Seattle, Washington. Seattle and New York were the outposts of this new genre. Determined to challenge Seattle's reputation as an overly polite society – Kurt Cobain, Nirvana, and the new screechy masters of Grunge Music performing at The Crocodile Cafe in the Belltown section of Seattle - dovetailed perfectly with the nearby caravans of slam contestants airing their works in down town taverns and laundry mats.

In the movie "School of Rock," Jack Black tells his young students that to become successful rock musicians they would first need to tap into their "anger." More than rock, grunge, rap, or hip hop – Slam lyrics are purely defined by each author's sense of outrage. The gritty performers are left to succeed or fail without the use of props, pyrotechnics, music, or percussion. And the audiences are anything but polite.

A Slamtrum

More children died today.
Murdered. And each time one
is plucked from our view of
another precious life denied,
we shake our heads, we call out the
"Who Would Do Such A Thing?"
We denounce the weapon used,
and we swear to be
thorough about wringing the
motive from the madman,
before we snuff out his lights
"because, god damn it,
there HAS to be a reason!"

There has to be a reason.
And in our need to be
good and thorough, we will
strike down and disassemble
the lame reasons we have been given,
until we have eliminated
every B.B., bullet, box cutter
and sharp rock with time running out, as
increasingly the child killers are children themselves.
And in our need to be thorough
we will even kill the children
who are killing the children,
soon as we extract the cold hearted reason.

When all the sharp pointed
objects and projectiles have been removed,
only then will we sound out
the madman whom we have hand
bell rung loud the REAL reason from,
and then we shall hear
about not having been held,
about not having been wanted,
about not having been taught,
about our not reading and being read to,
about not fostering curiosity,
nor reverence for our bodies,
nor consideration for all living things
as part of the whole.

Still, he is a monster,
a madman,
a nut job, a freak,
not good like us.
His words are whack
and cannot be true.
We have wrung his motive.
We have rung his bell
probably too loudly about
Life is War and War is Life,
about how we've bloated
every minute of every day

with things, Things, debt and
more things, and how the pressure
to pay and the pressure to buy,
push our mindfulness,
caring, reverence and regard to the side.
Now children are killing children,
and still you ask "WHY?"
And, "who would do such a thing?"

Remember as a child?
Remember the feeling?
Remember that kiss?
Remember believing that real life
was all about this?
Shut him up!
Put him away!
His bell is too loud
we have been told.
We can't un ring his bell
we have been told,
and we been told,
and we HAVE been told!

SFX: BLOOD CURDLING SCREAM

6
Freestyle/Rapid Fire

FREESTYLE WORD ASSOCIATION is the act of 'pouring out' on paper whatever springs to mind – immediately, spontaneously, as it occurs. Rappers are quite good at this, as are automatic writers and those who are able to channel other personalities.

Evangelicals do it when they throw themselves into a trance, speaking in tongues. Don't fret about making sense of what zooms out of you. This is a healthy bit of lawful anarchy.

Be brave and unconventional. Switch off your filters for the moment. Feel the liberation in exercising this part of the brain. Become unshackled from constraints and habits and well... brain washing. Try it! Ready? Take a deep breath...

Brain Free Mystery

Are you the man my father
Sent to take good care of me?
Monterey Cypress where great whites idle,
Where sailors in their sheets and sails,
Tack and hike in white capped gales,
Muddied men no match for
Bay wind swales,
They saw their efforts scuttled,
When just upon the inlet stern
An eerie sound made us turn,
Upon the last words of the
Maiden bow, strangled by
A leeward, "Are you the man
My Father sent to take good care of me?"
All calm now along the hot batches of Esalen.
Henry and June, and Anais Nin,
Tropic of Cancer she begins
Nasaling in the Big Sur Eucalyptus.
Big moon time,
Coast Highway rhymes,
Headlights dimmed on Bond's DB 9,
Bald kisses, near misses, the Michelins
Hold their high speed glide.

From Bixby Bridge to surf board tide,
Then Paso Robles, flooring it to
Simeon through every curve and
Every swerve, a date with Mr. Dean's
Last ride, just in time, Hearst Castle wine,
She whispered in quiet majesty,
"Are you the man my father sent
To take good care of me?"

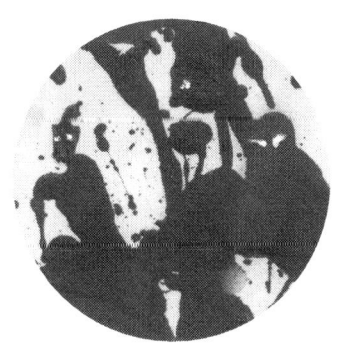

Ant and Elephant

"Is it strange? We did not see either. Both occupied the room. The diminutive and the outstanding. Magic says only the arrogant can be swindled as they ignore the agitated, the tired, the lowly. The Illusionist knows how blind are the ego grubbers to anything larger than they – and all that is meek below their feet. Strange, Wonderful, Weird. You and I can decide to reduce the elephant and grow the ant, so that love can be seen, somewhere in the middle."

Today's Fragmented Inspirations

. . . as obsolete as swing dancing.

Bill: Compose a symphony entitled, "Raw Furniture" – a sonata of sounds made by chairs dragged to different pitches.

Bill: Write this poem, "Woman On Top."

Good word: Horticulturist

"I found myself free-falling through Time."

Good word: Dilettantism

"I could seize the imagination of others, because I myself was seized."

Bill: Write this poem, "Man Without A Country."

Bill: Write this book, "Surviving America: A Resistance."

"He looked for a name, but found only a human digit, floating in the penumbra."

Good phrase: Upwellings of Emotion and Danger.

Bill: Write this book, "Ghost Writer's Valedictorian Speeches."

"I am as interested in the Meanings, as I am in the Facts."

"Imminent extinction, threatens my identity."

Good name: Marsden

"Dealing with cancer taught me the power of not getting bogged down by one event."

"Who's counting whom, and who's sleeping where?"

"The elusive goodness. . ."

"It is always there, except when you really need it."

"He vanished in the wisp of a souped-up mini-drone."

". . . taking refuge in my citadel."

Look Up
(the beginning of yet another children's book)

DIXIE and PIXIE and GERALD and BROWN
were simply three kids and a dog
from a really small town.
Dixie was Southern, from 'Bama or 'Loozie or 'Sippi,
or some place that had snakes on the lawn.
Pixie was puny, tiny as a pebble. Small.
Small as a book mark, and a good thing,
CAUSE THEY READ BOOKS ALL THE TIME.
Red Headed Gerald read too, as he was told
that reading books is what red heads do.
Brown didn't need to read. Dogs don't read.
BECAUSE THEY ALREADY KNOW THINGS.
Brown was bigger than Dixie the Southern girl,
and Pixie the tiny girl, and Gerald too.
Brown knew to PUT A LEASH ON THEM, and
lead them around, since his friends were
always reading, always looking down.
His three best reading friends
COULD ONLY SEE THE GROUND.
    (to be continued)

Letter Out Loud to David Mann

Dear David,

am roasting one of my usual late night coffee beans.
still trying to pull off this land scheme in Montana.
still trying to farm myself out as an escort, tour guide,
and connoisseur of nooks and crannies.
still trying to put together an
underground restaurant-coffee house.
still trying to make money in Arizona real estate.
still trying to write poems and short stories.
still trying to fuck old girl friends
who most enjoyed fucking.
still trying to send love to lost ladies
who are never convinced.
still trying to keep my cat 'Hoover' from dying,
so that he can travel to Arizona,
Montana, Dakota, and then Ohio.
still trying to believe in believing.

                        Love,
                        Bill

                      — Wednesday, July 23, 1975

Nine Thirty P.M.

The Grand Tetons, a skier's jump to your twin inhale, a breath too loud, rebel farmers' triggers pulled, someone precious goes to jail, we walk the ledge – your atlas lips like sand and trampolines, how close conquistador's westward look, two bodies close as fault lines, slabs repelling ivory Stonehenge monoliths, your tight dress lipstick leaves a skid. Loyalty and honor catch 'The Fall,' two victims of good manners, two titans breaking away from easy, trading lust for friendship, big and deep without cliché.

Not mountaineers in league with Cook and Peery and Sir Hilary – we only base camp here, fearing thin air where crimson violet nippled orbs jut through the cumulous. Best cross country slide through your sweaty canyon cleavage causeway – look out! They sway to safety with a heaving, pendulous sigh.

What did you dream in your parallel life? Are you inevitably self-esteemed as in this languid dance of you in me?

The spongy jaunt across smooth mother's stomach plains, a drink at your umbilical tide pool, where you were born and where you gave birth. We torched a match and danced this place, a tribute to your mother's will, then we rolled into your short-haired forest.

Lost! Lost! No light falls to the ivory floor, struggling to hack through the bush, and then discovery! A color emblazoned image blocking our path through the wiry wilderness. Mesmerized by the needle dyed turquoise and heart line of the thing, we cut and shave and trace the image. Bear! Bear! And there, motionless for hours we have time to speculate:

"What powers does it possess? Why does it reside HERE?"

On Hirsute's Cliff we stand atop your dripping place, the dew of you slides us down to Forbidding Cave, slippery fantasies lured to musk, ancient creatures petrified in your resin. We climb out to a fleshy ravine, whose warm slopes fold onto itself.

Two thighs. Two ridges forming the way. Rambling down the left archipelago not wanting to think your peninsulas must meet, or that lost will stay lost. Existence risk on, for what I believe I think I know of you, your imperial valley sashays towards an equal coastline leg, hurdling over finger lengths, exposed like redwood roots. So this is the Amazon.

When did you learn your toes could tie a sheep shank, half hitch, a hang man's noose? Not wanting to become Fall prey, we leap your foamy chasm, foot-to-foot, once again delaying intimacy's death.

Inspirited, we gallop into a sprint. Exhilarated, no governing gravity down the Water Girl Coast. Home bound, down your Ensenada, Santa Monica, Venice Beach, feeling the pull of Mendocino and Big Sur's reach, nuzzling and spooning hand across your arm to First Breast Breach. We know the way, nothing sunrise can teach. We are relieved. Here, you, out-of-body, prove we were not deceived. Again we are all with one and love retrieved.

Adventure ending with one last moon, sand under hoofs, we will be home soon. Gallop. We gallop. Did Love's need send us galloping to keep our love from going remiss? Even if it was but finger running, skin surfing, toe touching bliss? Now, the way you cinch behind me as we imagine to gallop tells me it is true, that no one can love me, no one like you. So from now until forever these little things I'll do.

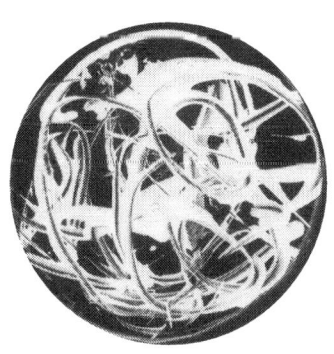

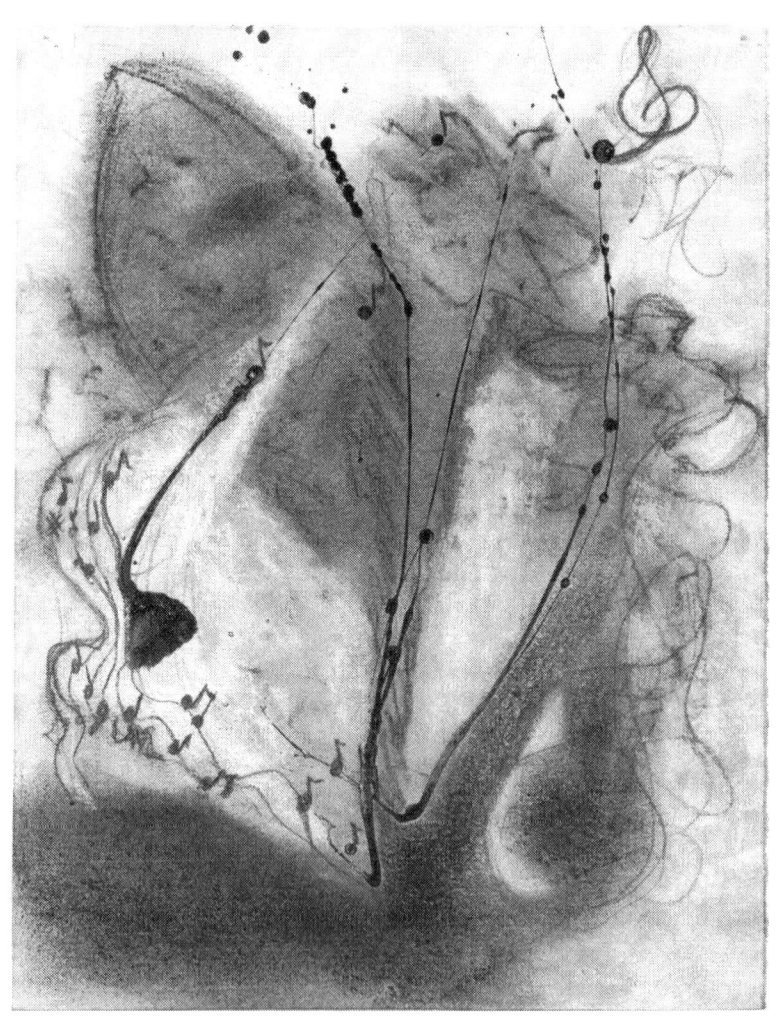

7
Song Lyrics

THE COMPACT MUSIC Dictionary,
compiled by Marilyn Bliss, defines 'Song' as
"A short poem with a musical setting..."

Perhaps there is a musician reading this
who cares to put her/his notes to my words.
Let's create SONG!

Love Passing Through

You worry that
my love for you
is passionate, addictive
but just passing through.

Don't you know that
I'd be long gone
if only that were true.
Don't you know that
no man can collect
a woman like you.

A real man knows
when a real woman
comes along, he's gonna pay for
his sins of long ago.

Nothing I can say,
nothing I can do,
Real Life's about
proving love, and
I'm at the back of the line
tryin' to get back to you.

You fret about the fragrance;
wasn't the one you picked for me.
Oh precious darling,
is there nothing I can do?

I'll be any smell you want me to be,
I'll be the scent of you.

You tell me
I'm a billboard man,
looking for a billboard woman,
perfect in every way,
can't you see I adore everything about you,
last year, last night, every hour of the day.

You and only you
are in everything I do.
I don't need a fantasy,
it's love simple love,
love of you and love for me
our fairy tale is real if you'll let it be.

Cheap Song

You don't love me anymore.
You don't love me
like you did before.
I've tried everything to
bring you back through Love's door.
But so far,
you don't love me anymore.

You know I hate to see you cry.
You cried for more blues
in the desert sky.
So I fill the clouds
by crying out loud,
and not a word of thanks
as you drive by.

When the rains finally came
you said it was a shame
you could not see.
I promised you my eyes
if only you'd love me.
You worried your wet shoes
would lose their glow.
I throw down my shirt
wherever you go.

You don't love me anymore.
You don't love me

like you did before.
I've tried everything
to make wedding bells ring.
But so far,
you don't love me anymore.

Some people wonder
what's in it for me
this yearning for you, this insanity.
They don't know you,
the you I adore.
They don't know how
you loved me before.
"Yes," they all say, "that was yesterday,
but she don't love you anymore."

You don't love me anymore.
You don't love me
like you did before.
I've tried everything,
I've pulled on every string.
But so far,
you don't love me anymore.

All the Way Down
(half-assed blues)

Many years ago in 1973,
a man in pain was crying,
propped up against a tree;
got on my knees to listen,
his eyes were made to glisten,
and then he said to me,
"If you're gonna do a man in,
do him ALL the way down;
nothing lower than a woman
who only fools around."

REFRAIN
Got the Blues, getting badder,
got the blues, getting sadder,
got the blues that hurt without a sound.
Got the Blues, in a bind,
not the half-assed kind,
and this time she's takin me all the way down.

Now I'm up, now I'm down,
stirred in your stew, beginning to drown,
Thought I paid my dues, then you came a calling
with your half-assed blues;
now you got me falling half way above the ground,
you might as well take me all the way down.

You're angry, you're beautiful,
don't know what I can believe,
another twirp on your arm,
another trick up your gown,
doubt that you will grieve
as I go all the way down.

This thing between us is growing old,
Love's dark addiction
is getting big and bold.
You come in Love's affliction all over town,
maybe this time you'll spare me,
take me all the way down.

Cars in the street, people in the park,
slop in the gutter, clouds getting dark,
some are watching movies, some watch the news,
just as I was changing, high above the ground,
she kissed me saying, "You only paid half your blues,
then my heart rearranged me,
and I went all the waydown.

Andy Warhol Song

According to my iPhone
thousands died out there today;
but being on the digital
tells me I'm O.K.,
and my mocha java tooty fruit
gets me through the day.

I need to buy a business suit,
looking good, going out to play,
sorry Martin, Malcolm, J.F.K.,
this is now and you were then,
you need to get a little zen,
ain't it time you went away?

    REFRAIN
He looks like Andy Warhol
the way he combs his hair,
he shows himself quite randy
in his underwear.
The beginning of distraction
that cockcrow derriere,
America loves its selfies,
its narcissistic air,
check the mirror, drop a bomb,
the country doesn't care.

I came upon a crashy,
everyone was dead,
a shot of me and them
for the YouTube cache'.
"I'm sorry for your loss," I said,
and continued on my way.

I'm sure the world is awful
but MY world is here to stay,
so stick with social media,
the message stays the same:
"Never touch a stranger,
and always look away."

Hungry for some multi-task,
at the super highway café,
"What you want?" the server asked,
"some 'friending' or frappe?'"
two gigabytes with chocolate,
and there was no delay.

So Pretty, So Poor

Somewhere south of nowhere,
where the big animals roam,
and you're too far gone
to think about home. . .
where you no longer
wash the wild pigs from your hair. . and
you're just about to that dark place
where you no longer care.

She shimmies through the hovel
the rubble, the late night trouble
in her unsoiled green pastel."
She carries red shoes in a basket,
across the bloody, muddy apron of death,
gracefully through hell's bad breath,
to the only dry dock
of your bad judgment.

And all you can say is. . .
"God you're pretty!"
desperate to see at least
a little bit more,
and all she can say is. . .
"Then God is pretty. . .
pretty but poor."

REFRAIN

Pretty, pretty, pretty, pretty,
wary man full of pity,
stuffed with guilt
and feeling shitty.

When he gets back
to the comfort of his city
he'll be changed,
no longer a bore.

But the place that changed him,
and the woman he now yearns for,
will still be pretty, so pretty,
so pretty. . . so poor.

— April 30, 2012

Sittin Out, Lookin In

When the sun gets up
in Wheaties land,
he paints with his palette
as best he can.
No glory,
no story,
just a brush in his hand.
He's a Picasso, a Rembrandt,
he's an Angelo, a Van Gogh.
He's an outsider,
but his disasters on canvas
trump their best of shows.

    REFRAIN
Sittin out,
lookin in,
another day passes
while the great unknown
start over again.
Next time, Life,
when you decide who wins,
look for someone in the shadows
who took it on the chin. . .
sittin out,
lookin in.

She's twenty five,
with soft painted toes,

not quite the girl next door.
She's rough,
she's tough,
the gritty stuff,
wore lipstick since she was four.
She's Marilyn, Marlene,
Madonna at the door,
but everyone who meets her
knows she's really much more.
Cause when her men are put to bed,
she becomes a nightingale
working with the poor.

REFRAIN
Sittin out,
lookin in,
another day passes
while the great unknown
start over again.
Next time, Life,
when you decide who wins,
look for someone in the shadows
who took it on the chin...
sittin out,
lookin in.

So many millions
feeling the hurt,

ground down by big money,
into the dirt.
Who gets to live?
Who has to die?
Your soul is the passport
to the big ticket ride.
So here we are
on the double edged knife,
it's time for you to notice
we're still here, Life. . .
sittin out,
lookin in.

FINAL REFRAIN

Sittin out,
lookin in,
another day passes
while the great unknown
start over again.
Next time, Life,
when you decide who wins,
there'l be someone in the shadows
who took it on the chin. . .
sittin out,
lookin in,
sittin out,
lookin in. . .

2007 – 2013

Song on the Shelf

You're my soft place
and you're my rock;
the first to forgive me,
you get me out of hock.

Can one woman be so many things?
You defy, you never falter.
Hope it's not too late,
be the end to all bad dates,
I love you lady Gibraltar.

You're the dew
in the morning glisten,
you're a breath of golden air,
you're the sounds that make us listen,
you're the feel of baby hair.

And when the world
moves in on me,
with no place left to go,
you ask me what I want to be,
you're my window to the soul.

Everyone has an answer,
every heart holds a song,
a little magic left to reach for,
when all the light seems gone,
you help me see where to go,
you're my window to the soul.

The Way

I put my nose
into a long stemmed rose,
as the sun laid me down
in old Sedona Town.
I was pretty darned sure
awakened by its allure,
I had suddenly got
a whiff of things
my teachers never taught.
Two thirds of a life
survived by a gun and a knife
in foreign lands,
I was pretty damned
good at taking lives.
Living as I lived,
one eye open
with my door ajar,
people say I'm lucky
that I got this far...

    REFRAIN
Life so fragile,
life so fierce,
an old, old woman
never forgets
how to cradle another
woman's baby dearest
out of harm's way.

A fire dies and new life soars,
written in blood
no matter what they say.
It's the Truth.
It's the Circle.
It's the Bear.
It's Tomorrow.
It might be Today.
One thing's for certain,
it's Life's Way. . .
it's Life's Way.

Came Home
Thursday, Thanksgiving Thanks,
a break from improvised bombs
and mortar tanks.
Then Black Friday barged
through dawn's first light,
the sound barely gone
that true religion brings,
lines around the block
to buy the latest things,
gas guzzling shoppers
storm trooping the doors,
grappling for bling
in all the box stores,
"Medic! Medic!" I screamed,
too late it seems.

When the stampede thinned out
a woman lay dying
on the showroom floor.
I could feel my voice
rising as I dragged her away
from the credit card hordes,
"So THIS is what we're fighting for?"

When I get back to foreign soil,
away from grills and
London broils
to the victor go the spoils,
over endless body parts
we will roam, churning
blood and guts to oil
in the desert sandy loam.
And what will you
be doing brave patriots
as we destroy these
people's homes?
Will you paste those yellow
ribbons on your shiny
petrol cars? Will you pay
the war lord murder drones,
to do your killing from afar?
Will you now divorce these things
while truth still has a chance
to ring? Or will you cast aside
this fragrant rose in spite of
the hope it brings, married instead
to your store bought things?

REFRAIN

Life so fragile,
life so fierce,
an old woman
never forgets how to cradle
another woman's baby
out of harm's way.
A fire dies and
new life soars,
no matter what they say.
It's the Truth.
It's the Circle.
It's the Bear.
It's the Sea.
It's something the eyes can't see.
Hell, it's whatever
you want it to be.
No matter what they say,
It's Life's Way,
it's Life's Way.

2012 - 2013

8
Obits

"The Hard Part Is Over"

(Biographical fragments of famous people
most of whom you never heard of)

I GET SO busy living, that I sometimes forget the dead, whom helped me along the way. Every October in the Mexican tradition of Dia de los Muertos, I trot out 'The List,' as well as the tequila and frijoles.

The New York Times noted in its 2012 Obits, that roughly 155,000 people die between each printing of the newspaper, and that The Times will only publish obituaries on 1,000 of them per year.

Most of my fast and famous friends existed out of the limelight and under the radar. This feat is not as easy as it may sound. The Times would have been graced giving ink to any one of the outrageous individuals poetically honored in this chapter.

Decades ago I began eulogizing some of these 'prefer not to be publicized' characters (in some instances BEFORE they reached the inevitable milestone), as a way to appreciating their heft.

Touching Ziggy
(for David Bowie)

Not a single note of transcendent rock
unstills the pain
as death puts us through one more
of your changes.
We disavowed heaven when you fell,
we danced inside
your stardust gaze;
we pranced as heathens to
your fashion fame;
we crowned you Prince of Oddity.
Now we stand impossibly quiet
with you in our imagination,
honoring your irreverent place;
your moveable musical castle;
your exotic grace.

        As shared with Anugito Ten Voorde
                — January 11, 2016

Harris
("Git, Obit")

When it used to
never mattered, what
the prices of things
would be,
an said what I will,
an goe'd with mustard
an steam over others' hills
with none the asking.

They sayed I
was clever,
ahead of the time,
for ne'er goe'd round,
ne'er left ne'er right – I
barged through,
forged a straight line.

I am done now
an in my bed,
slowed by a heavy hand
rude as red,
too weak
to bout the whispers,
they paint me one d'em
idiot sublimes.

No fears 'cept one.
I fare resigned, chained the great plow
circle to the dark, the big undone.
Take ye fun
carrion to the eddy,
mocked in lime,
but please, please don't
end me a horrible rhyme.

— December 25, 2012

The Pillars of Grace

You've passed on this eve. Some would say, "Finally."
Your victims – your enablers, prayed at your side.
I too, spent the day with you, but far away in detached
thought, wondering as deeply as your morphine sleep,
whether I would surrender truth and recite something
trite when the final word arrived. Blessedly the Angel
of Love reminded me not to pretend that monsters
don't exist. Together, observing your departure, we
packed the alms you requested but were never able
to say: "Thank you," and "I am sorry."

          — July 29, 2014
            5:10 P.M.

Monte's Ashes

Some of the people he hurt
gathered to finish the dead business.
The ashes, then the cemetery plot,
fees and services. I declined my 'share'
of the corpse, thinking it too hypocritical
to spurn in life then pay for decencies.
He could be buried in the family plot
we were told, but only if the urn could
be planted on top of or below one of the other
relatives. None of the living volunteered.
Then came the remembrances. I thought
hard, deep, and long. Like most predators
Monster spent many hours divining himself in
the mirror. It was the best I could do,
so I remained silent. A strange wondering
blanketed my thoughts – a question whether
there was guilt required for not expressing sorrow.
Bad memories began to interfere, my mind
sorting them like so many recent
revenges of the Arabs and the Jews, of
humanity wronged everywhere in every Time.
Ironically, the man in the ashes relished
just such confusion. So again,
I allowed the alms to stay denied.
And I worried for the World.

— August 11, 2014

Leuken

You are the most unassuming person
I ever met. And probably the kindest.

So politely you asked me to take away
your daddy's pistol. I now know you
are going to do it in a way that leaves
little mess.

Thanking me in advance for being with
you at therapy, is likely a red herring.
You have been in unsoothable pain
for the entirety Your parents say you
have lived your graceful life truthfully
but without complaint. You have made
it delicately clear you don't want to be
saved.

Today you played peekaboo, grinning
behind an alabaster column at the top
of a grand stairway. Then you returned
a book of poems, one of them marked.

I'm on my way to your house, up the I-5,
but I'm late for our movie date. Should
I be worried?

— 1995

Piece of a Prayer

We ask you to revenge
our unhealing wounds;
we do not want to
know what you do
when no one is looking.

To us, you are
the considerate, deliberate,
dangerous kind;
our young sisters
wanted to be with you.
Our childish limerick jests,
discerning yes, but
did you really care?

Years of drinks later,
so many losing bets;
we still ask you, fearfully,
our unexpectant hope rising,
to win for us.
For the eternal time
you sigh,
"Truth? Or Dare?"

— Late July 2013

Noreen

He was a beautiful man
in every way. I believe
I am right to say that,
not just that his hair
was clean, and straight,
and that he looked chiseled
and svelte and good.
His face lines led you to
his earned life lines,
guarded by green eyes that
did not blink much.
He had a reputation for
keeping a gun close at hand,
even as he slept. I presumed
to know things about him,
as we traveled through some
states in step with each other.
He as a man who built things.
Me as a sellerman.
He looked good in his builder's belt.
He once said he liked Somerset Maugham.
He was a beautiful man.

— 1992

Randy Rhyme

A fast flying Ace
named Randolini,
wore a special red cap
on his beany.
With a great sonic boom,
he'd enter a room,
and out would pop Cathy,
his genie.

— October 2009
(revised November 2012)

Gottschalk

He seemed to materialize weird and wonderful happenings. One of these in particular stays with me and has been retold many times. A housemate of ours burst into my bedroom one evening dressed only in a silk robe and refusing to leave until he be allowed to read Allen Ginsberg's HOWL in its entirety. He did this on one of those rare occasions where I actually had female company. Like any real man I felt the need to expel the trespasser.

Aside from the minor brawl caused by the epic poem and its reader – Gottschalk had his own reasons to be frustrated with the great poet Ginsburg. He had just suffered through a week of teaching Beat Poetry to a vocally unappreciative audience of intelligent but bigoted soldiers at the Naval Post Graduate School in Monterey.

The following morning, dressed as usual in his plain black professor's suit and tie, Gottschalk plodded to his car, not looking forward to classroom duties, which at the moment appeared so unrewarding. Intuitively and for the first time in his teaching career – he played hooky, driving instead down the beautiful Coast Highway.

Upon reaching the Bixby Creek Bridge, Gottschalk again acting on intuition turned left off the highway, away from the Pacific and into the woods (perhaps he was simply looking for a place to relieve himself). He walked a ways and was drawn to the moaning cries of a man in distress. There slumped Allen Ginsberg at the base of a giant juniper, in pain and cradling a broken arm! Steve provided water from his thermos and prepared a sling from his white dress shirt.

The short version of this story is that a grateful Ginsberg returned from the hospital with his new Samaritan friend, and attended Gottschalk's class the next day, personally commenting on each officer's exam essay from the week before. After some lively Q and A, the controversial poet activist received a standing ovation.

Gottschalk's reflection on the matter was to point out, "Right Wingers are more apt to be outspoken. Subsequently they are more able to change their thinking in the face of what's real, than their quiet, shadowy, phony counterparts – the Pseudo Liberals." Because of this truism he warned me, "cities like Boston and Seattle will be the last to shed their prejudices." Wow!

— 2006

Clark
(for the Great Randolini)

When good friends
tire of the usual shit,
when the best of people
sincerely ask for it,
the rally cry in full refrain,
"Let's all meet in Randy's Brain!"

Randy's Brain
is home to paper routes
and Indian scouts,
fast planes and electric trains.
Randy's Brain
forgets wars and bores,
and rude sounds banging
on the weary-go-rounds.
Randy's Brain tunes in
birds and butterflies,
all things with wings
across the sky.

Let's meet in a place
that cleaned its space,
for lemon and water
and sugar cane,
Let's all meet in Randy's Brain!"

For the Great Randolini

When good friends
tire of the usual shit,
when the best of people
sincerely ask for it,
a rally cry fills the refrain,
"Let's all meet in Randy's BRAIN!"

Randy's BRAIN
is home to paper routes
and Indian scouts,
fast planes and
electric trains.
Randy's BRAIN
forgot wars and bores,
and rude sounds banging
on the wearygorounds.
Randy's BRAIN tunes in
birds and butterflies
and things with wings
across the sky.

Let's meet in a ~~████~~ place

— October 2009
(revised November 2012)

Dugan

Good Time Charley
died alone at home
in his favorite chair.
He sat upright
in his suave suit,
tanned, with all his hair,
still a hint of Richard Gere.
That's the way
they found him there.

— 2007

Danny's Epitaph

Good Time Charley
died alone at home
in his favorite
chair, ~~flannel~~ ~~with feet~~ swanky ~~one~~ suit
~~tagged~~, ~~and thrown~~ ~~on with roses~~ with all his hair
still a ~~bit the~~ hint of
Richard Geere, That's the
way they found him
there.

Nov. 2007

Good Time Charley

You looked so good
and Hollywood,
in your undertaker's suit,
thrilling women
with your kissing skills,
there, in outlaw town
where so many hearts
get broken, even your friends
sleep with one eye open.

That game we played,
"When I die..."
we toasted our brains
man to man,
"...please make me life like,
Digger Dan..."
You whiskeyed sentimental
late at night,
your Saint Paddy's Pride
retreating behind curtains,
shedding tears over tissue,
tubing, and formaldehyde.

"When I die. . ."
you completed,
"make certain I am seated,
yes, sitting up. . ."
How fitting the ten year roost
ended for you, with everybody gone
just the other day.
Be of good cheer, Charley,
you were erect in every way,
there in your chair,
looking pretty much
like Richard Gere.

— 2008

For the Memory of Dixie

Jaci Wilson,

I could not pass by this splendid hollowed out Jack Russell book. My thought is that you can fill it with all kinds of good Dixie Stuff – so called DIXIE MEMORIES AND MEMORABILIA. Given that precious Dixie's days of adventure here in this realm are probably limited, I ask that this big book be my contribution to Dixie's Legacy. Dixie is the sweetest, the fun lovingest, the smartest, the toughest and most fearless Jack Russell. DIXIE IS THE BEST DOG I EVER KNEW.

— June 15, 2014

Cover
(House of Ruth)

Mother of my good friend Jim,
made me swear briefly to look in
on him,
"until he can hang by his
own two limbs,
and that should prove enough."
Her savvy brain and stitcher's faith,
lifted Jim to a higher place
within the church of strength and grace.
Sewn Jim; the fabric of truth and tough.
And that will truly be enough.

— 2013

Chip

I am afraid to write anything about you.
I know the power of words — even mine.
This is not about you.
And not about me.
It is about not "embering,"
Which you are not.
It is your new word.
You are creating
More life than you are killing.
You are not embering.

— May 22, 2015

Split Second Decision

When I heard that
one more had died
I took a drive in the woods,
thinking of things to say
prosaic, things good enough
to exalt my dead friend,
remembering something he
impressed earlier about the importance
of dying beautifully, masculine, upright,
and with a mythical smile.
Right there I rounded
the corner of Hope and Worry,
thinly reassured that it was still Fall.

     — October 29, 2012

Slatkow

This friend of ours
died a little in October.
Stubborn, lonely, and afraid.
On Halloween. Can't remember
him ever putting on
a costume, but the last
years he wore a mask.
He got eulogized a lot
because he went slowly,
with each lessoning bite of food.

Each of us made the
man whole again,
with our memories.
A funny thing he did;
a weird time; a profound experience;
recalling a tendency; a man story;
a woman story;
his anger; his politics; his kindness.

Ironically, the strain
of getting intimate with
this historic figure, made us
better at being close to others.
In a perverse way
it became one of the aspects
of his greatness. The dying man
caused in us what he could not be.

Frankly it scared the shit out of me,
that a larger than life person
could shrivel this way.
Then... the spirit of his former self
must have danced its ass off,
because it rained where it had not rained,
and one of those triumphant rainbows
children draw, arched itself
over his stomping grounds.

"So what would the bastard
say to us now, if we could have a word
from his side of the fence?"
That's what I wanted to know.
And then his rainbow
came and sat next to us.

— 1989

The Longevity

I knew a man
named Stan, barely.
We never spoke
in our sketchy crossing.
In this unreliable realm
his aged Tree stood
tall, and deep, and thick
and wide. I gorged myself
from the man's cauldron eyes,
the unfazed broth
of life earned;
and that has made all the difference.

The Longevity

I knew a man
named Stan, barely.
We never spoke
in our sketchy crossings.
In this unreliable realm
his aged tree stood
tall, and deep, and thick
and wide.

~~The man's eyes~~
I drank wide open
from the man's eyes
the unfazed broth
of a life earned,
and that has
made all the difference.

Wirtz

Dear Mr. Wirtz:

It has come to the attention of my under-stimulated staff that Northern Arizona Hospices, Inc. should immediately avail itself of your brand of patient insurrection, for better care outcomes. Under your direction and consultation we are prepared to recruit: Nurses from Nevada's Friendly Colt Ranch; Nude contortionists from Casino du Soleil; and of course male cheese cake lounge dancers. Furthermore we are prepared to substantially up your standard 'Holy Terror' Fee, but only if you will include the music of your local 'Musical Madams Club.' Please add 10 % to the dollar amount if your female medley also includes your sister who lives in thecavehouse.com, and whom we understand can assist with our new Radiated Medical Marijuana Seed Research Program.

As you probably are aware, most of our patients have Alzheimer's. We are convinced however, after advance word about your Sierra Vista Method – that a rowdier, Lee Marvin/Earnest Hemingway beer and whiskey style 'Cancer Man' such as yourself – is more what the doctor ordered to shake the brain plaque loose in these 'shuffle boarders,' in order to dispel with current lack luster medical theories.

Anticipating that you will turn down this desperate, yet generous Offer unless we provide pickles, booze, and accommodations for your Thousand Member Fan Club – we have commandeered a fleet of mothballed busses, fully equipped with porta-potties and open bars.

Awaiting but not expecting your reply to this matter, I am wishing you well.

        Dr. F. Mann
        V.P. of Advanced Procedures
        Northern Arizona Hospices Association

P.S. To raise the necessary funds for the above, we have taken the liberty to acquire and sell your trademarked and patented HURLEY BURLEY BEAR HUG, WHISKER RUB DOLL.

CC: Crested Butte, Homer, Kodiak, Guaymas, Bisbee Brewery Gulch Chapters of the 'Warm Water Fish' and the 'Alaskan Crab Bait' Societies.

— 2013

Cathy's Randy

There was a man,
a man's man,
a man calm and confident,
not needing anger;
and he got the girl by
being real, sharing adventure,
never danger.
It is later now, way beyond
a wow or wows anew.
The girl is still the girl.
The man is still the man,
a man's man,
the bravest man I ever knew.

— 10/09 revised 11/12

Self Eulogy

Crisp, quiet, earnest,
as I planted some
colorful and easy
tomatoes, as the earth gave
mulch to mustards and
marigolds,
I came across a surprise,
sullenly mourning for myself
within the constraints of
what I already knew.
So THIS is the meaning of
life, these free samples of
demarcated wisdom for
all who pass by within
the crosswinds and the
heather,
tilling the soil of years I've
had,
Life isn't necessarily good,
Death isn't necessarily bad.

— Late July 2013

9

Lucid Dreamer

NEARLY EVERY MORNING between 3:00 A.M. and 4:00 A.M., I am launched from my bed by a lucid dream. At times I am 'dream drained' by the intensely vivid story lines.

This has gone on for years. Here are a few that remained in the vapor.

Two American Pastimes
December 24, 2009
3:30 A.M.

I am in an audience somewhere (Seattle I believe), at a classical music recital, a public lecture, or a comedy club. My date reveals to those sitting around us and no one in particular – that I am writing a book about Baseball. This evokes a collective "hmmmm. . ." in surround sound, much like the noise on nature shows, when the beekeeper holds a microphone inside the swarm.

After a certain amount of personal anecdotes and some statistical jibber jabber, a fellow immediately behind me reveals that he and his two buddies in attendance (at whatever this event may be) – are players for the Red Sox. All he wants to talk about is Game 7 of the recent world series with the Yankees, and how his role in one of the sport's most fantastical moments ". . .resulted in breaking the 'Curse of the Bambino.'" I try to sound knowledgeable by injecting that I have a copy of the 1919 contract releasing Babe Ruth from the Sox to the Yankees. But this guy is too caught up in his World Series flash back, and cuts me off with a hand to my shoulder.

"So they announce the starting line up for the new inning," he prattles on. "Me of course. . . and that guy. . . and that other guy. . ." he continues drearily on. "Why can't I remember their names?" By now he is flying deeper into his own personal fog. ". . .and I'm thinking I should meditate on something powerful, so I can lead off with a hit." Then he lowers his voice with an ominous effect. DON'T TRY TO BE MORE REAL..." He leaves the entire punch line hanging, and all of us seated within hearing range hanging with him.

"Do you mean 'don't try to be more real than you already are?'" I toss into the mixing bowl hoping to elicit something more digestible.

"NO!" he snaps back. "...don't try to be more real..."

Before his words have time to settle appropriately with the floor dust, I leap completely from my auditorium chair, turning in a circle amongst the small group of us involved in the befuddling baseball exchange.

"I have just changed my mind," I blurt out with some sense of urgency. "The new book is NOT going to be about baseball. Since the stocks of Starbucks and Green Mountain Growers have been exploding – the new book will be called COFFEE PEOPLE!"

The Sounds of Baseball
(Seattle, Washington)
October 28, 2008

I am traveling with a Japanese vs. American exhibition baseball team. It is part of new international effort towards something named the 'Anti-Language.' Suddenly I am cast into the starting line-up as me, a 60-year-old player amidst a legion of 20-somethings. It is the bottom of the 9th inning, two men Out. I hit a measly grounder to First Base, but no one is there. So I scamper to Second which is also vacant. On I go to Third for a stand-up triple.

After several amateurish attempts at to lure my foot off the bag, the Japanese team calls Time Out. This continues for more than an hour as the opposition sequesters in an administration building a block or two away.

Deciding to investigate, I am using my baseball bat as a walking stick. I find myself in a grapefruit grove. Whimsically I hold the bat above my head as I walk, causing balls of grapefruit to fall on me.

Finally I locate my Japanese counterparts and inquire as to the game delay. Excitedly they explain that they have been using the time to work on a theme – a slogan for the Anti-Language campaign.

"Well. . . what about us Americans?" I reply indignantly.

"You? You don't need one," they explain.

"So what did you come up with?" I prod a bit impatiently.

"WE GO!" they shout in unison.

"Jeez," I think to myself with disgust, "and I'm worried about how to slide into home plate without breaking any bones. . . ."

Getting Things Done vs. Who We Are
August 2010

It's journey time. Mostly on my hands and knees. Out of a dirty slimy dark old building, through a window. Then into the light, shimmeying down the smooth bark of an ancient fig tree, the differing heights of its trunk and branches enabling me to explore rocky craigs, narrow paths, mountainous terrain – all butted up against the venerable tree. The surrounds appear to be a burst of natural beauty: a river, a mossy hillside, a pastoral valley leading to a seascape.

The fig trunk leads me to the base of this mighty landmark where another trunk heads upward again, continuing my intended direction. As I stand between the 'wish bone' of my new friend, an enthusiastic black labrador leaps up at me. The dog is with a group of black men who are walking the other direction on the ground below – the direction I just came from, even though from a different set of twists and turns.

"How high can that dog jump?" I ask his seemingly friendly owner.

"Seven feet six inches," the stranger answers without needing to think about it.

"How'd you measure that?"

"With a high jump bar," the black man replies matter-of-factly. Then dog man and I go for coffee nearby. Looking up I recognize Wesley Snipes with his back to us. A new clothing tag is dangling from Snipes.

My coffee mate removes it without the actor noticing.

"I like it here. I wish I could stay," I say after a bit, "but I need to keep moving. I don't know why. But I do." The stranger and I don't exchange names. We simply enjoyed the moment without saying anything.

Moving towards the Ocean again, I am walking and crawling and inching my way along each twist and turn of the second arm of the massive wooden tributary. It leads me to the second story of a house. A man and a woman whom I vaguely recall from my time in Bisbee, Arizona – open a window to their living room and invite me to come in.

"In Bisbee I used to believe that politics was about getting things done. Now I believe it reveals who we are," I remark after some small talk while petting their wiener dog 'Charlie.' The friendly people in the house at the top of the tree ask me to stay.

"Thank you but nothing can stop me from finishing this journey," I reply. Their faces are kind looking but blank. "By the way," I add, crawling out the window on the other side of their living room preparing to get back onto the tree, "thanks for letting me travel for a while on the 'Inside.'"

Curiously I did not step onto the tree again. Instead I find myself about to be the featured speaker at an insane asylum luncheon. Apparently I am the only 'patient' at this weird reception, and my release from the place is dependent upon the success or failure of my presentation.

"I would like to quote from Vicktor Frankl's most important work," I begin. Unfortunately the title is nowhere to be found on the dust jacket of the book.

So I pause and they return to their food. This starting and stopping occurs three or four times without success at the title. Despairing somewhat, I put down Frankl's still unnamed manuscript, and attempt instead to summarize. Now I hold the undivided attention of the luncheon guests.

"Look, people," I blurt out from my insanity soap box, "let's face it. This is all about how we go in here and how to get out." The audience freezes as if unable to re-engage without learning my meaning to Life. "It's really quite simple," I then conclude. "WE MUST LIVE OUR LIVES RESPONSIBLY."

Time Delayed Exposure

Dream Poem
Sedona, Arizona, October 2011

When they peeped on us and
eavesdropped
from what was once the heavens,
easily peering through bright cold
skies and cumulus clouds,
and quilted fields,
veering down upon the tar and
gravel paths paved with
the pride of our fathers – knowing us better
than we knew ourselves – was made easier.

We thought OUR avenue skied down
the only prairie mountain.
It was but a hill.
She raced her nailed polished popsicle sticks
against mine. . . on this our decline.
They watched. They watched her
mat my hair and wash my hair
after tumbling me down.

She was my first girl.
She was a tall girl.
She was my first sled ride,
my first bike ride. . . my first kiss.
They watched. They watched as she

held my feet off the ground,
wheeling me down St. Joseph's Hill.
She galloped beside me hollering
"Remember how to fall!"

They listened to her lie.
She was a liar. She lied about her age.
"I need to, I'm big," she would
say while sitting on me.
They watched. They watched her
watching my eyes to be certain,
"puppy love certain. . . that I understood.

"Not that way little man," she cackled,
fisting a tuft of my hair
and pulling me onto my back,
down onto a lush, warm.
summer lawn belonging to
a North Dakota night.

"Look up, look up!" she urged,
forcefully showing my head
which way to look, so
willfully touching me.
"See? It's called Sputnik and
it knows EVERYTHING ABOUT US,
my little Elmer Squee."
She was way, way ahead of me. . .

FADE OUT.
FADE INTO. . .

My First Girl in a
pine box – a flag draped box
in a chapel.
Not in Nam twenty minutes
they took her without pause,
in spite of her protected lies.
She was a liar.
She lied about her age and
they knew. They always know. . .
they knew she would have
taught me there are more flowers
than prairie roses.
The many flowers of love.

They knew she would
not outlive her parents;
not bear them a shining moment;
not see more of the world, touch its people,
taste its food, revere its monuments;
not experience enough Time – its wounds,
its marvels, its subtleties, its wrinkles.
And yet? Maybe? Perhaps?
While I am allowed these awestruck things,
she will still be way, way ahead of me. . .
asking as they watch, they the Thou. . .
"Oh my doting boy, my darling bow wow wow,
where is heaven now?"

Here We Go Again
(Sedona, Arizona)
September 2008

Why does the tour bus only drop me off in Bisbee? This time the guides point to and yammer about every nook and cranny except Main Street, where I am hoping to surprise all with my resume as the Master of Main Street. Alas, they deny my ego any such opportunities."

Somehow I fall in with a group of locals who enjoy each other's limitless conversation. At some point two of the women are walking away from the rest of the pack.

"Hey girls," I bark. "Get back over here!" The chatter instantly goes quiet. One of the renegades is standing over me with her arms crossed.

"Now here's a man with attitude," she muses sarcastically. She walks away. I am transfixed. She is definitely a hipster with geeky glasses and matching patented leather purse.

I fall asleep in my clothes and stroll with one of my new buddies to work. He is a wiry man in thin linens, and wears a bow tie. Twice I ask him to pronounce the name of his business. Each time he gestures toward the overhead sign. Each time it is lost on me.

"Why don't you just call it LIM, JIM, AND GUNGA DIN?" He ignores me.

The rest of the day is spent attempting to lure my 'New Girlfriend.' Geeky Girl and her matching purse seem to hold no agenda except to suggestively strut her stuff up and down the main thorough fares. From there she segues to the alleyways and drainage paths. I run ahead of her along the way, playing dead, dressed only in underwear. With indifference she continues to step over my corpse.

"O.K.," she relents after finally stopping and straddling me, "let's go home. We arrive at her place only to be greeted by a disapproving mother, which immediately drains all interest from me.

Menudo
(Cottonwood, Arizona)
March 30, 2007

    Traveling with an invisible female companion. I only know that she is there and that traveling together we have come from the other side of an arduous journey to the top of the mountain. So high that we speculatively muse about smelling coffee beans and burlap bags. Chile? Peru?

    Not actually a mountain top. More like an apex or the tip of a peak – a space so constricted it can provide for but a handful of cheerful villagers, who spend their time foraging for their singular community enterprise – a restaurant. This uniquely magnificent provider is perched in the tasty open air. It sits upon its mountainous diminutive stage of adobe block ruins, carefully embroidered with sand, grass, and button sized flowers.

    It is approximately half an hour before sunset. The eatery's pinnacled patio cantilevers from its dizzying height, peering out hundreds of miles, and looking down its Andean slope for thousands of feet. Above us and immediately below us are just enough alabaster walls and terra cotta roofs to fold us into the arms of everything that we are not.

    Apparently we are expected. The sky high café contains only one table! The sounds of Nirvana –

a mother gently scolding her young one, two lovers laughing, old men talking, klacking kitchen commotions – all subside as we are seated.

    Our server is dressed in a black suit worn thread bare, white shirt and thin tie, places a soft white linen napkin in the lady's lap. Observing that I have an erection tenting up my slacks, he places an equally fine textile on my lap without fanfare. The man is thin and statuesque, a human tower in this place; an ancient soul perhaps, with his bluish grey leathery skin and those alien eyes that see without looking. He vanishes in the same unobtrusive manner as he appeared.

    Returning momentarily, our host quietly places two bowls before us, each one on a serving plate. The courses are accompanied by solid silver spoons. The vessels and plates can only have arrived from another world and another time, formed from colossal pearls. With continuous measured resolve the grand server ladles the only item on the menu: steaming hot soup made of animal intestines.

    A slow moving cloud passes through us, cooling the broth with its fog. For me it is the most peaceful moment of a lifetime.

Jeff Bridges
(Cottonwood, Arizona)
March 11, 2009

    Jeff Bridges asks me to be in a film with him. "It's going to be called THROW ME A KISS," he explains. "It's a Baseball film – an anti-Kevin Costner baseball film," he continues. "This thing is going to have a lot of gore and splatter, and galactic sized explosions. You know – the kind of movie young people will want to see!" Bridges is very animated about his movie pitch, telling me to zip it each time I counter that apple pie baseball and blow up the world scenarios are never attached, and typically occur far apart from each other.

    I wake up laughing. But the more the dream's residue causes me to itch during the day, the more I see goofy possibilities in what Jeff Bridges had to say. Now I am convincing myself that BLOW ME A KISS might fit as a sequel to Bridge's waking life unheralded but excellent feature film, THE AMATEURS.

    Even better, the entire cast of THE AMATEURS probably will gel perfectly in the new story line. I can do this!

The Eric Schmidt Dilemma
(Sedona, Arizona)
March 22, 2013

From a dream sequence in which a handful of us are attending a technical conference headed by the Goggle genius himself. All of us are meditating in a small circle. At some point Mr. Schmidt embraces me, sobbing "Yes, yes, yes!" I awake at four in the morning wondering WHY my dream catcher snagged this and the following garble, of which I have little comprehension and even less interest:

VIRTUAL DIGITAL CHALLENGE

How to make, cause, or enable tangible goods, services, etc. to travel at the same velocity recognition, and ease – as WORDS do.

Even the Schmidt Conference presentation images of the Tangibles are so much slower as to be cumbersome, unwieldy. . . late (typically, at best, they might finally arrive by Federal Express). Consequently the human words are speedily launched from the brain by way of time altering gadgets. Tangibles on the other hand – are bulky, retarded, and subject to the whims of chaos, as they snail along in their clumsy cocoons – pitifully attempting to catch up or rendezvous. . . with the words and ideas which proceed them.

At this moment the Eric Schmidt Challenge remains: How to properly logistic words and their tangible representatives TO TRAVEL TO AND ARRIVE AT THE SAME PLACE AT THE SAME TIME.

Long Lost Good Friend
Steve Chesney
(while camping cross-country in my mini-van)
2010

Now I am an 'Off Broadway' song and dance man, with top billing at a fading side street New York theatre. It's a two person show I do with a younger unknown actress.

The unglamorous marquis showcases BILL MANN, but the last letter is heavily smudged and barely readable. Inside, we perform but one musical number, Stevie Wonder's "For Once In My Life," which we perform over and over like a recording that never stops looping.

Tonight there is only one customer in the auditorium. It is Chesney! After the performance we squeeze each other in a vigorous and lengthy embrace.

"You finally came!" I exclaim. "You finally came!"

Chesney and Julie
(Location and Date Unknown)

INT. CHESNEY'S LIVING ROOM – DUSK

JULIE is clawing at freshly laundered clothes piled on the couch, and is throwing them into a suitcase.

          JULIE
      (mascara awash)
   How dare you not cry!

        CHESNEY
(shirtless, wearing jeans, watching
     her from a chair)
  I'm outta tears today.

          JULIE
(unsuccessfully clearing her vision
      with a towel)
Please, don't let me do this alone – say something!

        CHESNEY
(nodding grimly toward the suitcase)
You'll bust the guts if you stuff anymore in that.

          JULIE
(pulling a mangled scrap of paper
 from her blouse, and reading aloud)
"How is it possible that the telephone can make

the things you describe, so REAL?"

CHESNEY
(pointing, defensive, desperate)
You swore you'd never go through my things.

JULIE
I'm the one you love, stupid!

CHESNEY
Now THERE'S a word you've beat to death.

JULIE
Please. PLEASE tell me why. Why did you keep her letters?

CHESNEY
What a week. One moment it's white cake and rice... the next you're packing your crayons.

JULIE
Our ages have finally caught up with us, haven't they.

CHESNEY
Yeah.

JULIE
(arms crossed, bending over, heaving whale-sized tears)
Oh, Chez, it's broken, real bad.

CHESNEY
(rising quickly)
What is? What's the matter?

JULIE
Our Dream – remember?

CHESNEY
(easing back)
"...A runaway strawberry blond, took up with an excellent ex-con..."

JULIE
(continuing the romantic limerick)
"...She gave up her running, he gave up his gunning..."

CHESNEY
(in a droll tone)
"...and love went on and on and on..."

JULIE
(packed and at the door)
Well, I guess that's it then.

CHESNEY
(growing uneasy)
Jules?

JULIE
(attempting to be big about it)
Please, don't... don't get up.

CHESNEY
(down in the mouth)
Where you gonna go?

JULIE
(softly patting her heart)
Wherever you go to get these things fixed.

JULIE EXITS QUIETLY, WITHOUT CLOSING
THE DOOR, AS CHESNEY'S EYES GLISTEN.

FADE OUT TO: MUSIC AND CREDITS

THE END

No Name, No Place
(Location and Date Unknown)

To a fellow in a natty looking suit, who works for my lawyer uncle in a patent firm:

"Why can't we just leave?"

"Because we are system emoters."

"Oh, yeah, I see what you mean. I'm skating on thin ice around here."

After a little pause I add, "So I'm forced to say my "Buoyancy Prayer.""

The Ravens, The Real Estate, The Room, The Roof
July 25, 2014

This occurred as my last REM before waking, while wearing a PAP MACHINE mask. I have just purchased a narrow building in an unknown town, that needs extensive restoration. Probably an old church, frame masonry, wood floors, and filled with sunlight. It is a captivating bit of architecture with a five-sided, mansard flat-topped roof. The interior ceiling is beyond high, maybe thirty feet tall. Inside, fifteen real state agents or so are wandering about, exploring the building's space, holding champagne glasses, chatting it up. Because of the vast open space and no furniture, the voices sound animated and echoey.

A stairway attached to a wall of the former church leads to an upper grassy terrace defined by tall trees on three sides. The interior floor level contains tall double doors which open to a smaller, narrow, disheveled garden enclosed in a gated metal thicket fence.

One of the sales people calls me out to the upper terrace where he/she extends an arm and says, "Watch." Out of the trees swoops a Raven, which lands on the agent's outstretched landing post. The bird is tattered and dusty, but still robust. It stays for a moment then returns to the trees. "Let me try," I join in. When I hold out a stiff arm, the large bird dives toward us, but lands again on the other person. "Maybe it's that red shirt you are wearing," explains the agent. Then another equally ragged looking Raven flies down upon us, this one landing on my horizontally extended 'branch.'

The birds go back to the tree and we return to the party. While milling around, I find a small room with lots of windows. Standing there I am filled with pleasure and hope. I look into a mirror on the wall and see myself from the side. The mirror reflects the profile of me as a ninety to one hundred year old person. Then I wander into a second room, which is nearly dark. As I go into the darkness – the entire building begins to vibrate like one of those old electric hand massagers, at very fast r.p.m.'s. "Here, let me help you," urges one of the agents, who then flips a switch on the wall, returning the place to calm.

Briefly I mingle again with company employees. Nearby the former owner is boorishly going on about all the efforts he performed to make the building "a national landmark." It is almost as if he is deliberately testing the limits of the rest of us, who cannot escape that the structure is beautiful, but blatantly in need of repair. "Yes," I blurt out of nowhere, "but have you stood outside lately, and looked down upon the roof?"

At some point I walk out to the lower level garden and through the metal fence. This takes me to an adjacent property. An elderly couple are standing there, passively acknowledging me. They nod, but do not shake hands. "I want to be a good neighbor," I say, smiling at them.

"Look, there's Shotsie," the older man says in a heavy eastern European accent, "but he doesn't see us." The older woman muses, "Oh, that's easy. Just give him the finger." And so she does.

10
Children's Stories

Perhaps coincidentally, perhaps not – the artists, musicians, writers I have known embrace childlike qualities loaded with the assumption of immortality. Instinctively children realize early that they need to hitch their organic powers to life lessons, before they can journey outward. Their entire beings are screaming, "Teach me! Teach me!"

Through observation, the fortunate ones trust their heavy handed, lethargic, weary minded adult custodians to provide little more than food and shelter.

Instead – quickly and naturally – they latch onto charismatic animals, supernatural creatures, imaginary friends, and venerable old people. These specially appointed guides, like the children themselves, don't allow schedules to impede their Time Travel, nor gravity to frighten them from taking giant leaps.

Children's Stories involve learning while suspending beliefs. But think about this: Are they more for the children, or are they all about the adults?

Paula Goes to the Pound
copyright 2013

Illustrated by Alexandra Colombo

Paula was a poodle,
a very artistic poodle
who very much loved to doodle.
She loved stroganoff and strudel
and anything with noodles,
but mostly she loved her Mother.

Paula's mother, Cathay,
danced for the local ballet.
Cathay was pretty in every possible way.
She ate healthy and exercised each day.
She didn't have much money, which was okay.
Because life was rich with little Paula.

Paula doodled everything she saw from the stoop.
She drew planes flying loops,
she sketched kids playing hop scotch and hula hoops,
she penciled the woman with the nylon stocking droops,
and her mother Cathay serving ice cream scoops.
And...Paula drew the stranger man in the little white van.

"Come closer," said the stranger with the very friendly face.
"No," answered Paula, "I'm not to stray from this space."
"I've got cookies, and noodles,
and for your mother some lace."

"No, I still better not," insisted good Paula, "just in case."
"Can you help draw this lost puppy
who can't find her place?"
Then Paula came closer – and that was a mistake!

"You tricked me," growled Paula, as he threw her inside.
There she saw some other scared dogs
who were 'going for a ride.'
"See what happens when your parents rules
you don't abide?"
And all the captured dogs cried, and cried, and cried.
Cathay searched the streets for Paula, from side to side,
as dogcatcher stranger man drove the dogs to the pound.

The pound dogs laughed at Paula's French beret,
her lashes, her curly 'do.
"We're throwaway dogs, all black and blue.
We're nobody's with no purpose, and nothing to do.
Welcome to the dog pound, 'toutalootalou!
In here, the same thing might happen to you."

The pound was lonely, dark, and deep,
not a good place for a dog to sleep,
even if you knew how to count your sheep,
or prayed the lord your soul to keep.
"Tomorrow," Paula comforted the ones who weeped,
"I'll do a portrait of each of you."

Meanwhile Cathay oh so worried, found at the curb,
Paula's drawing of the dog catcher in detail superb.

Cathay cried out for help in a newspaper blurb,
she was beyond fear, she was perturbed.
She clamored before the judge, she would be heard!
But still she lacked money to save Paula.

All day and the next Paula drew dog portraits galore.
She drew Rex Retriever fetching big things,
small things, things outdoors.
She drew Bobby Bulldog nipping a boar,
she drew Wolfhound Hank robbing a store,
and Colleen Collie watching the door,
and none of Paula's new friends believed
Paula's mother would come.

Paula kept drawing, she felt such a rush,
"I've got to finish before Mom rescues us."
She penciled Johnny Greyhound chasing a bus,
and Ricky Rat Terrier making a fuss,
Great Dane posed regal, patient, completely nonplused.
That kept Paula from fretting
whether Cathay would finally arrive.

Cathay kept dancing for minimum wage.
Her pirouettes wowed people each night on the stage,
but her heart was heavy knowing Paula was caged.
Totally desperate she sought advice from a sage.
"I'm sending you help, it's completely arranged."
That's when Cathay's doorbell rang.

"My name is Motorcycle Mike,

I wear tattoos and leather, and drive a motorized trike.
I'm an Aussie for justice, anything animal like.
When people have problems, my sympathies strike.
So if you aren't afraid to be a bit unladylike,
let's go and get Paula, let's get her tonight!"

The line was getting shorter for the Jail Portraits Club.
Paula drew Sam Schnauzer, Betty Beagle,
the Boxer, the Pug,
Pekingese Pete, Charlie Chihuahua,
Alley Dog Amy with hair like a rug,
Rosey Ridgeback who wore rouge on her mug,
Dogue de Bardeau, and Napoleon Mastiff
stomping a bug.
Finally Paula said, "My work here is done."

Then did Shotsie shout,
and every barred window he did scout,
he heard a motor sound that made his ears twitch about.
He belted his big voice
through his charming little snout,
"Someone's come to bust us out!"
And Paula began packing her easel.

Motorcycle Mike used his bolt cutter
and lock pick just right.
Cathay on his shoulders, held a steady light.
Sophia Setter and Vizsla Val led the four legged
prisoners into the night,
for all who loved freedom, a most beautiful sight,
full moon lighting dogs, all taking flight.
The moon's shadow guided Cathay. . . and Mike. . .

and Paula all the way home.

Next morning the police came like bloodhounds,
wearing a scowl,
"Gather up your things, and come with us now!"
"But how did you know we did it?
How? Tell us how!"
"Fifty dogs missing, forty nine returned
for breakfast chow.
That means the jail breaker is the one
still out on the prowl."
So off they went in handcuffs, and leg irons for Paula.

The courtroom was packed with wagtails.
Someone kind and wealthy posted all the dogs' bail.
The ballet patrons came hoping to see Paula prevail.
Neighborhood folks and their children stood on the rail,
then the judge loomed over them all, big as a whale.
"Silence!" he barked.
"Prepare yourselves for what I say."

The judge cleared his throat so many times,
that kids in the court read their nursery rhymes.
A nearby church went through its chimes.
Law-dog bailiff flipped a dime,
"Heads they go free, or tails they're mine."
But finally the judge was ready.

The judge's murmuring words filled every ear:
"Well liked ballerina... fine artist Paula
of very good cheer...
animal rescue... no money... needs her mommy dear...

war hero leather man with nothing to fear."
And then... Here's my decision, so everyone draw near."
The place go so quiet you could hear hearts beat...beat.
..beat.

AND THEN...

"Community Service. No jail for you larks.
Ballet Cathay, you will dance in the park.
Poodle Paula, you will paint children, but only till dark.
Motorcycle Mike, you'll give free rides
to the zoo," he barked.
"I hereby make it so, by signing my mark."
Then everyone cheered for fairness and liberty!

"Wait!" roared the judge as the aisles got clogged.
"No one leaves the court without claiming a dog.
From this day there shall be no underdogs.
ALL dogs shall be declared SPECIAL DOGS.
And today THIS DOG (he pointed at Paula),
shall be TOP DOG.
Now go home do-gooders, go home and do good."

And that's the story of Paula the Poodle,
known far and wide as the dog who could doodle,
who loved her mommy and Mike and her strudel.

When asked what top dogs consider caboodle,
"I only know," she laughed shyly, "I do love my noodles."
But mostly Paula loved her mother.

THE END
(for now)

Sarah's Voice
copyright 2013

Long ago in the Right Now, under the brimming over of the 'Who Gets What,' emerged a band of children, moving along the Good Path.

"Where are you traveling?" asked other little ones when they saw the march of the Good Path walkers.

"We're following the sound of Sarah's Voice," they answered cheerfully. "Can you hear it too?"

And the children along the Good Path could hear her voice.

"Would you like to come with us to find Sarah's Voice?" the new friends asked.

And so more children joined the band of other children in search of the Voice. Walking along the Good Path and collecting more and more children as they went, caused the number of children following the sound of the Voice to grow larger and larger, spreading wider and wider across the land.

The swarm of children grew so large, people all over the world began to notice. They called it, "The Children's Crusade to Find Sarah's Voice." And at each place along the Good Path, still more and more children said they too could hear the Voice, and so they also joined the gigantic march.

As the children walked together along the Good Path, marching and singing and whistling and playing, it became only natural to ask each other, "What do YOU hear when you hear the sound of Sarah's Voice?"

Some children said Sarah's Voice sounded like a Mom or a Dad, or a Big Sister, or an Aunt, or an Uncle, or a Grandma, or a Grandpa reading stories to them, while being tucked into their beds.

Other children said the Voice sounded soothing, like a singing teapot, or popcorn popping, or a kite flapping in the wind, or a soft breeze, or musical notes, or a thousand other things.

Still other children walking the Good Path together said Sarah's Voice sounded like the bears, and bees, and birds, and rabbits, and lady bugs, and all of the friendly creatures from their most favorite books.

Every child had their own idea of what Sarah's Voice sounded like. But they all agreed that Sarah's Voice sounded like safety and warmth, and strength and kindness. . . and love.

Finally the Good Path led the Children's Crusade to a steep meadow climbing up a perfectly round hill. And from the very top came the beautiful sound of Sarah's Voice. So the many, many, many children who had traveled so far together to find this place... sat quietly next to each other, all around and up and down the hillside, so that they could listen more closely.

Then the warm Voice filled the inside of more bubbles than any child could count, as the bubbles floated down from the top of the hill, touching each child as each child reached up to touch them.

"Praise Be To Children," the Voice began. "You traveled the Good Path instead of worrying about the Who Gets What." And all the children murmured with understanding.

"You are all here together, so nothing more needs to be said," the Voice continued. "EXCEPT..." And the many, many, many children leaned forward to listen better.

"No matter where you are today, tomorrow, and the day after next," the comforting Voice spoke to them again, "BELIEVE IN THE SOUND OF YOUR OWN VOICE."

Then... at just the right moment all the children gathered around the sound of Sarah's Voice, stood up together. Holding hands with each other they returned along the Good Path leading to each of their homes, all around the world.

And all the parents were so happy to have their children back home... that for one giant magical moment they stopped worrying about the Who Gets What.

And anyone who listened closely that very night...
could hear all of the big people asking all of the children
around the world, a most wondrous question:

"WILL YOU TEACH US THE SOUND OF
SARAH'S VOICE?"

THE END
(for now)

Saving the World from Boredom
copyright 2014

Before there were fire trucks or Swedish pancakes or
baby rattles, or milk in a bottle, or
music or didgery sticks, or whiz bangs...

Before all that the world was mostly quiet and things
inside the world were mostly still...
...unless... you were lucky enough to blow in the
wind, or be carried by the rainy rivers, or be warmed by
a fiery fire started by lightning.

BONNIE BUTTERFLY and BRAINY BOY were
lucky in those ways. When they weren't busy blowing in
the wind, riding rainy rivers, or warming themselves
around lightning fires – they visited each other every day
to describe their favorite things.

"I like getting my feet sticky with pollen," said Bonnie.

"I like my thick, telescopic glasses that find the furthest
stars," said Brainy.

One day after boasting of wonderful things they each
liked about themselves, Bonnie and
Brainy Boy ran out of their favorite things to talk about,
and they fell silent. The two befuddled friends thought
about their problem. They thought... and they thought
some more. They were afraid to say it – but each of them

silently worried about being captured by the
BOREDOM MONSTER.

And just when they were about to run and hide from
the Boredom Monster, Bonnie Butterfly came up with a
big idea.

"Since we've already described all the wonderful things
we each like about the world around us, why don't we
say all the wonderful things we like about each other,"
she said in a perky way as she fanned her gorgeous
butterfly wings in Brainy's face.

"That is Brilliant!" shouted Brainy Boy. "Why didn't I
think of that" he pondered.

"You would have sooner or later, I am sure," Bonnie
said, like good friends do.

And THAT was the beginning of saving themselves and
saving the world from the Boredom Monster. Because
everyone knows that things about each other are so
much more exciting, than things about ourselves.
ENDLESSLY more interesting.

THE END
(for now)

The Dog that Rode Horses
copyright 2013

Back in the Day, but not too far from the Before Now, lived a most average dog. People say this average unforgettable dog looked a lot like your dog – small but not too small, tall but not too tall, average just right with your favorite colored eyes, and of course the dog had two ears and a tail. The average special dog was average perfect for every boy and every girl. In fact, the dog's name was EVERYDOG.

Even though Everydog was just your average, loveable, dog next door, Everydog became known far and wide as "The Dog That Rode Horses."

Wherever Everydog went horses would get on their knees, allowing Everydog to jump up to their backs and ride away, just as if the two very different animals had been friends forever.

Many pictures and stories told of Everydog making children happy in every town, by riding horses at the circus. . . or in parades. . . or in the movies. Everydog even did horse work on ranches and became the star attraction at rodeos.

No one seemed to know where Everydog came from, even though everyone comes from somewhere. But no one asked because they were so busy watching the many tricks and tasks Everydog could do with horses. And no one seemed to ask why Everydog always looked around when high up on horses, as if this average wondrous dog was searching for someone or something.

Indeed, because Everydog was so popular with children and people everywhere, it was assumed Everydog had no problems. Besides, as Everydog passed through each little town, this most average great horse rider never needed to worry about food, or water, or a place to sleep. As you might guess, Everydog preferred to stay with the horses in a barn, or in a corral, or under a shady tree.

Everydog could not speak words. But when Everydog barked, people believed Everydog was saying things like, "I'm just your average ordinary dog," and also "I never met a horse I didn't like."

Of course, being so loved by little horses, and big horses, and work horses, and the horses of Kings and Queens – Everydog traveled to every place in the world where horses lived. And being an average good hearted dog, Everydog continued to entertain children and their families, and deliver things by horse to needy people. Every so often with the help of horse friends, Everydog even saved a life or two.

One day in the life of Everydog, a day Everydog will never forget, a horse whispered something in the average dog's ear. Suddenly Everydog stopped, listened carefully to what the horse was saying, then jumped onto the whispering horse's back and rode away, faster than a train, and at least as fast as the wind.

People who tell this story, say that horse after horse carried Everydog across rivers, mountains, and onto big boats traveling across the oceans and across the seas. The brave and tireless horses seemed to know just where to take their good friend Everydog.

Finally... somewhere between the waters of Goody Good and Nicey Nice, just above Warm Cinnamon Porridge, and along Kindness, Caring, and Tickely Toe Trail... Everydog who had been lost and searching the whole time of his worldwide adventure... found the place from where he came.

Unless you are a horse, no one will ever know the secret of how the horses knew where to take Everydog. But everyone – every child, every horse, every dog knows that we all come from somewhere – that someone somewhere loves us, or is waiting to love us like no one else can.

And the best place of all places to come from... IS HOME.

THE END
(for now)

Tiny Templeton
copyright 2013

Cats are strange. Tiny Templeton will always be remembered as the strangest cat that science, common sense, or the world has ever known.

In that happy place where grandmothers and grandfathers live to be the age of turtles, and parrots, and elephants – Tiny Templeton was born the teeny weeny size of a mouse. Tiny Templeton was born at the feet of Fernie Gablowski.

Fernie Gablowski was still alive at one hundred three years of age. That made her the longest living legend of Saint Luke's Home for people who lived as long as the trees, especially beautiful trees like redwoods and the wise old bristle cone pine.

Because Fernie Gablowski was the oldest and the wisest person at Saint Luke's, the other grandmothers and grandfathers wanted to know her SECRET.

"Be nice to Tiny Templeton," she would tell each of them, "and he will show you my Greatest Secret." And then she added, "but not for more than one hour at a time."

So they did. Each of the 'gray hairs' at Saint Luke's began to invite Tiny Templeton into their little homes along the hallways. They petted Tiny and held him in their laps, and they fed him warm milk, and they let him take naps in their rocking chairs.

Naturally all the good food, love, and affection caused Tiny to grow into a healthy, bright-eyed, shiny haired cat. All the 'old ones' at Saint Luke's had made a new friend.

Just as they had agreed with Fernie Gablowski, Tiny Templeton went freely from room to room along the hallways of Saint Luke's, visiting his many gray haired friends – but never staying with them for more than one hour.

One hour each day, was plenty of time for Tiny Templeton to listen to the wonderful life stories of the gray hairs. And they had plenty of stories to tell. Because each gray hair had lived a long wise life.

Then one day no different than any other day, and for reasons no one at Saint Luke's could think of. . .

Tiny Templeton went into the room of one of his many gray haired friends. . . and he refused to come back out. Even after one hour.

One hour became a day. . . and that day became a night. Tiny stayed on the bed of that particular gray haired friend, giving comfort and listening to stories until that person drifted into permanent peaceful sleep, passing on to wherever turtles, and parrots, and elephants, and redwoods and bristle cone pine trees go when the time is just right.

After this same thing happened two or three more times, the gray hairs at Saint Luke's realized that Tiny Templeton's Secret was that he knew exactly when it was time for a gray hair to pass on to the next peaceful place.

Suddenly, Tiny Templeton's friends at Saint Luke's became afraid. They now believed that Tiny Templeton CAUSED them to pass on to the next peaceful place. So they began to shut their doors in Tiny's little face when he came to visit each day.

It became a sad time with all of the doors closed. The gray hairs became lonely again, because they missed sharing life stories with their best friend, Tiny Templeton.

Then Fernie Gablowski called a meeting of all the gray hairs, all of the grandmothers and all of the grandfathers at Saint Luke's.

"Tiny Templeton is NOT the cause of our passing to the next peaceful place," Fernie explained in a calm voice as she walked around the meeting hall. She held Tiny in her arms as she spoke.

"Tiny Templeton is here to warn us – to kindly let us know when that special time is near for each one of us. Tiny Templeton is here to help us have time to prepare and get ready for the next peaceful place."

Now the gray hairs could see that Fernie Gablowski was not afraid of Tiny Templeton. They now knew that she spoke the truth. And they were no longer afraid...

Once again the doors opened freely to Tiny Templeton. The gray hairs saw clearly the wonderful Secret of Tiny Templeton and his special purpose. It was a happy time again with lots of cat petting, bowls of warm milk, lap sitting, and storytelling. No one was lonely. And no one was afraid...

More time went by at Saint Luke's. Again, on a day no different than any other day, Tiny Templeton was making his usual visits. But on this day Tiny entered the room of Fernie Gablowski and he refused to come back out. Even after one hour.

After waiting and waiting, after the hours filled up the days and the nights that followed – the gray hairs politely entered Fernie Gablowski's home along the hallway.

And there... Fernie Gablowski and Tiny Templeton lay together in permanent pleasant sleep. They had passed on to the next peaceful place TOGETHER!

The very next day... the person who replaced Fernie Gablowski as the oldest and the wisest at Saint Luke's, looked down... only to find a teeny weeny cat the size of a mouse, born at her feet...

And THAT is why everyone knew from that day forward and all of the days that followed. . . that among all the good and mysterious ways of life. . . that both gray hairs and cats KNOW SECRETS.

And one thing is for certain: Cats are strange.

THE END
(for now)

What Does Bear Do in the Woods?
(a bedtime book)
copyright 2013

The Jibacanoe was visiting from the Land of Bleepy, in search of the mythical Bear found only in the deep dark forest. When Jibacanoe finally reached this special place he built a safe warm fire in a fire pit before the fall of night. Soon many animals who lived on the edge of the forest gathered around the warm fire to talk about the creature they feared the most.

"Where is Bear?" Jibacanoe asked each of the animals warming themselves by his fire.

"He is in the woods," they answered.

"What does Bear do in the woods?" Jibacanoe continued to ask.

"Bear is too big and scary, so we never follow Bear into the woods," the smaller creatures added.

"What do you THINK Bear does when Bear is in the woods?" Jibacanoe insisted, as he looked into the timid faces of all who sat in the circle of the friendly fire.

Rabbit spoke first. "If I was Bear, I'd look for carrots. Bear has big teeth like me, so I would chew things in the woods. Raccoon spoke second. "Bear has hands like me, so I'd look for fish in the streams as he travels through the woods."

Elk sat next in the circle, so he spoke third. When Bear stands up Bear is tall like me. So I would shake berries and seed right out of the trees."

Possum opened his eyes, cause he was next, so he spoke fourth. "Like me, Bear sleeps with ease. I believe he might hang from a thick branch in the woods, and pretend with his zzzzzz's."

"Bear likes my honey," offered the Bee, as Bee warmed on a rock, fifth in the circle. "If I were Bear, I'd make honey in the woods, in a big honey comb."

Wild Hog sat sixth in the circle, so he took his turn. "Like me, Bear's legs are strong and his jaws snap with a loud thud. So if I were Bear in the woods, I'd dig and I'd grunt, and I'd wallow in the mud."

Fox was slow and thoughtful before speaking his mind, but he was seventh and it was his time. "Bear is the only one with a nose that might or might not be better, because it is bigger than mine. If I were Bear in the woods, I would go were my nose goes."

Snake was eighth in the circle, so he spoke in eighth place. "Bear is curious like me. If I were Bear I would play hide and seek. I'd look for snakes on leaves, under rocks, and swimming across creeks. I'd hide where I thought no one would peek."

"All very good and helpful ideas," smiled Jibacanoe as he looked inside an old medicine bag that he wore around his neck. "I shall always consider you my friends for life, and that means for keeps. But I've traveled so far, and now that I have listened so closely to each one of you, I need to find out for myself. So I had better go find Bear where none of you have looked, into the woods so dark and deep. Please put out the fire before you sleep."

When brave Jibacanoe finally found Bear, Jibacanoe learned quickly what the other animals had not seen with their own eyes. Jibacanoe saw that all the creatures who feared bear were wrong about Bear. Bear was sobbing and making Bear tears so large that the ground was covered with water all around Bear.

"This is what I do in the woods," Bear cried out in his sobbing voice. Jibacanoe quietly pulled some moss from a nearby tree, to help Bear dry the sad tears. "I care about all the creatures in the woods, and I try to make sure everyone is safe and protected," Bear explained in a gentle voice. "So it makes me cry when they are afraid, so crying is what I do when I'm in the woods. To make it worse, whimpered big Bear. . ." I'm so big that everyone is afraid of ME, and I don't have any friends."

As Bear blotted tearful eyes with the forest moss, Jibacanoe thought and thought some more. Then. . . Jibacanoe said the words everyone everywhere likes to hear: "I have a good idea, Bear."

Before that day ended, in colors bold and bright,

Jibacanoe pulled all but one of the jelly beans from his special pouch, and made a giant jelly bean sign at the door to the forest that looked just right:

ALL CREATURES WELCOME
TO BEAR'S BIG FEAST IN THE WOODS.
YOU SHOULD ALL COME.
YOU REALLY SHOULD.

And so they did. Thanks to Bear: Rabbit got carrots, Raccoon got some fish. Elk received berries and Possum got a possum's wish. Bee got fresh safflowers and pollen for a honey dish. Hog got hog slop, and mud on the toes. Fox received new smells to enjoy with the nose. Snake learned a new spot to hide from all foes, riding on Bear's back, a place nobody knows.

Bear wore a smile. Bear got something too: a Jibacanoe jelly bean with stripes that looked like a rainbow all around, the first jelly bean of that color ever to be found!

The special visitor got up and left the party on that star filled night. The moon was big, showing plenty of light. No animal felt fear and none felt alone. Smiling Bear was surrounded by new friends who had grown sleepy. They all fell asleep before they could ask, "WHAT DO JIBACANOES DO IN BLEEPLY?"

THE END
(for now)

Bird. Wind. Tree.
copyright 2012

Long ago, when Summer, Fall, Winter, and Spring were first meeting each other, WIND was barely a child and was having trouble scattering the first seeds across the great prairies. Seeds of alfalfa. . . and wheat. . . and corn. . . and barley. . . and flax.

One day a cheerful bird came along and said, "I will help you, WIND." WIND was wild and messy. BIRD was orderly. In the powerful arms of WIND, BIRD was able to deliver each type of seed to the exact place for that type of seed. Together, BIRD and WIND made many, many seed deliveries, each to its proper place in the prairie fields, until the corn and the wheat seeds and all the other types of seeds grew into big bunches called crops.

"Now we are ready for People to come and build homes for their families, and to eat the crops and plant new seeds each year," BIRD said to WIND. But BIRD looked worried.

"What now?" asked WIND.

"We need something tall for me to sit in," said BIRD, "for me to sing from to let the first People know where the crops are." WIND and BIRD thought and they thought.

"I think I know the answer," smiled WIND proudly. Then WIND went away in a whoosh and returned with the biggest seed BIRD had ever seen. And from that acorn seed WIND and BIRD grew TREE. TREE was a big tree. TREE was a giant oak tree, reaching high for the pillow shaped clouds in the endless blue sky. BIRD built a nest at the top of TREE and sang WIND to sleep at night.

One day BIRD shouted to WIND, "I can see the first People coming!" And he sang and he sang. BIRD sang as loudly as he could. He happily sang the songs of the Meadow Lark. . . and the Robin.. and the Crow. . . and the Sparrow. . . until he was satisfied that the first People could see TREE, and know which way to go to find all the seeds that BIRD and WIND had planted for them.

Then BIRD looked worried again.

"Now what?" WIND said patiently.

"We need to help the first People," explained BIRD, "especially the Children," he further explained, "to know where to put things and be orderly while they wait for their first homes to be finished."

"Hmmm," said WIND softly, not wanting BIRD to be unhappy. "I think I have an idea." WIND looked all around TREE and then he said calmly, "Just whisper to me which of the Children's things go where."

When the first people arrived after following the songs

of BIRD, they were so thankful to find so much good waiting for them. And THAT is how the first new people met their first new friends, BIRD, WIND, TREE, and summer and fall, and winter and spring. And THAT is how children have always known the right places to put their things.

THE END

Other Books by Bill Mann

Paula Goes to the Pound

A very gifted Poodle teaches us that all Dogs are special creatures, even if they live at the Pound. Add a very determined Ballerina, together with a Veteran who has a noble sense of purpose—and you get an epic adventure story for children and adults alike. Readers will enjoy the colorful characters inside. PAULA GOES TO THE POUND is based upon actual events, brought to life by the dazzling imagery of internationally known Illustrator Alexandra Colombo.

Hardback, perfect bound • Full color inside • 8.5x8.5 inches, 28 pp.
ISBN 9780692631133 • $17.95 • Available as Ebook, ISBN 9780692588727

in real LIFE

A four year old boy wakes from a coma. Believing that the people rushing toward his bedside are not his real family, he begins a search for his true parents. Don't expect the usual coming of age story. In Real Life is a first person chronicle, of a thirty year journey about embracing life as the ultimate prescription against detachment and anti-social behavior.

Paperback 6x9 inches • 97 pp. • ISBN 9781466495203 • $17.95

Big Time Lessons from Small Town Poker Players

This fascinating up close and personal study (including photographs) contains the largest and widest depiction of the 60 million small stakes poker players in America today. See if you don't agree that this long overdue poker anthology takes the emphasis off the money, and puts it squarely on the character required to handle yourself at or away from the green felt jungle.

Paperback 6x9 inches • 428 pp. • ISBN 9780615155975 • $24.95

Made in the USA
San Bernardino, CA
30 October 2017